HOW TO REA

HAND

CW01668855

HOW TO READ CHARACTER

IN

HANDWRITING

OR

THE GRAMMAR OF GRAPHOLOGY
DESCRIBED AND ILLUSTRATED

BY

HENRY FRITH

Author of "Chiromancy; or The Science of Palmistry"; "Character in Handwriting"; etc.

WITH NUMEROUS AUTOGRAPHS, AND EXPLANATORY DIAGRAMS OF HANDWRITING SELECTED FROM VARIOUS SOURCES.

TYNRON PRESS
SCOTLAND

© This edition, Tynron Press, 1990

First published in this edition in 1990 by
Tynron Press
Stenhouse
Thornhill
Dumfriesshire DG3 4LD
Scotland

ISBN 1-871948-58-4

All rights reserved

Cover design by Beatrice Ling
Printed in Singapore by
Chong Moh Offset Printing Private Limited

CONTENTS.

How to Read Handwriting.

PREFATORY REMARKS.

IN the following pages there will be no ambitious attempts to explain existing and easily ascertainable facts. The science of Graphology, or the art of judging of character from handwriting, is rapidly becoming a rival study of Chiromancy, or Palmistry ; and as Graphology is the much more easily learned, we may assume that it will be the more popular as time goes on. As subjects of study become popular they require simpler modes of instruction to meet the wants of beginners, and of the busy ones who have little opportunity to devote to a new study.

In the following pages we hope to illustrate clearly the various stages needed for the understanding of Graphology, and to lay down the simple rules whereby all may, if they please, obtain much amusement, and, it may be, instruction.

"But," some may say, "what is the use of knowing the characteristics of handwriting?" Such a question has been put to the writer more than once. Of course, the same question might be put concerning any other study—Greek or Latin, or some more abstruse branch of knowledge. But an anecdote may supply the reason.

Some two years ago a barrister, well known in his profession, came to me with a letter in his hand, and asked my opinion of the writer. The correspondent was a stranger to him, and only a small portion of the writing was revealed with the envelope. As requested I seriously examined the writing and gave my written opinion upon the character of the individual, in confidence. For what reason my friend required such testimony I did not inquire. Some months afterwards the barrister again came to me and thanked me warmly for my delineation. He said, "I acted toward the man in the manner I judged best from your dissection of his character. He was a perfect stranger to me; and I may add that your cautions, and your readings of his characteristics put me on my guard; you have saved me a considerable sum of money."

Some readers may wish to know that my friend then and there invited me to (a very excellent) dinner. I never have regretted that diagnosis of character!

From this illustration it may be gathered that there is some utility in the knowledge of Graphology, and numbers of readers will find it a useful accomplishment. In some cases it may create distrust, and in some may even cause dissension; but the knowledge, like all others, will put us on our guard and enlighten our understanding. We may remember Wendell Holmes' division of the individual man into three: The man as known to himself; the man as known to his fellow-men; and the man as known to his Maker. By our study and practice of Graphology, we shall arrive at a much more correct conclusion as to a person's real nature and disposition than we could otherwise have done.

As I have already set forth in a lecture on this subject.

Graphology is "common sense," and before the reader has perused this little work, he or she will discover the truth of this. It is not necessary here to quote the writings of learned men respecting the possibility of deducing character from handwriting. When we find such clear-headed writers as the elder Disraeli, Goethe, Lavater, Walter Scott, and others, maintaining such possibilities, and bearing such testimony to the truth of the principle, we may pass on and accept it too. "The handwriting bears an analogy to the character of the writer, as all voluntary actions are characteristic of the individual." Surely, this is "common sense!"

Nevertheless, we must not expect too much from our study of Graphology. We must not suppose that it will teach us or tell us *everything* concerning our friends, acquaintances, or strangers. It is obviously impossible that a few lines of writing will inform us what is a person's profession, for instance; but it will guide us to the choice of a profession, if we study the tendencies of the absent individual from his writing. We may tell him he is most fitted by nature for such and such an occupation, because he has already evidently developed certain traits of character; and if he cultivate his gifts he will succeed in the line of life for which those gifts are *desiderata*, or at any rate useful and generally requisite. Let us, therefore, protest against those who assert "that a complete history of any one can be deduced from his handwriting alone." Nearly everything may be learned from a careful study of the hand by Palmistry, if conducted by an expert, but not by the handwriting, which will, however, give a very clear insight into a person's true character, his tendencies, temper, disposition, virtues, and vices. Mind, we do not say that he *practises* all these; we only say that his nature, his tastes, his temperament, incline him to such and such displays, and that, *au fond*, if not in actual practice, he is what we can discover by his writing.

Therefore, we maintain that handwriting will reveal the character *if the writing be spontaneous and unstudied!* Many people assume a style which is quite at variance with their true caligraphy. With perfectly legitimate objects too.

"Georges Sand," as is well known, wrote a masculine hand when contributing to the press in her unknown character;

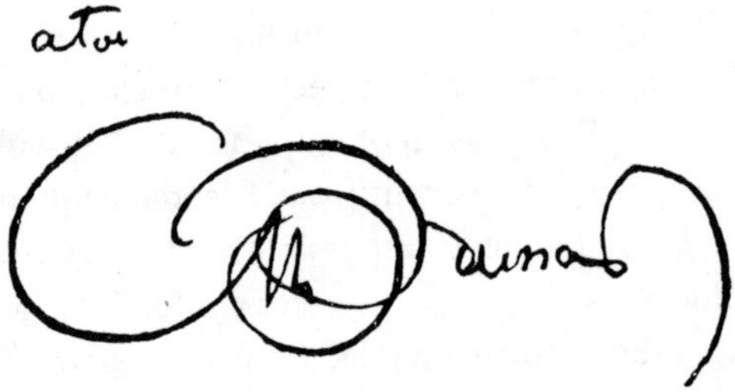

and the same difference is observable in the artificial and the natural penmanship of Alexandre Dumas. We give the two signatures, so that the real and the artificial may be compared. Some traits are common to both, but the adopted signature gives us no indication of the vivacity, imagination, intelligence and energy of the true man. The "swagger" is perceptible in the flourishes of both; self-appreciation is evident.

In these cases we readily perceive that the spontaneous handwriting is the only true test of character; and again common sense comes to our aid, and tells us this must be so. The unfettered, open mind discovers itself in its handiwork; we read between the lines. The man full of *finesse*, who, for certain purposes of his own, carefully conceals his handwriting, and writes in most clear and candid fashion when his nature is dissimulative, will deceive any one into a belief in his truth. But even he may be found out by a careful study of the individual letters.

A natural unstudied hand, then, is the only true test for character. Even the carefully honest attempt to make our "hand" as clear as possible may give a wrong impression

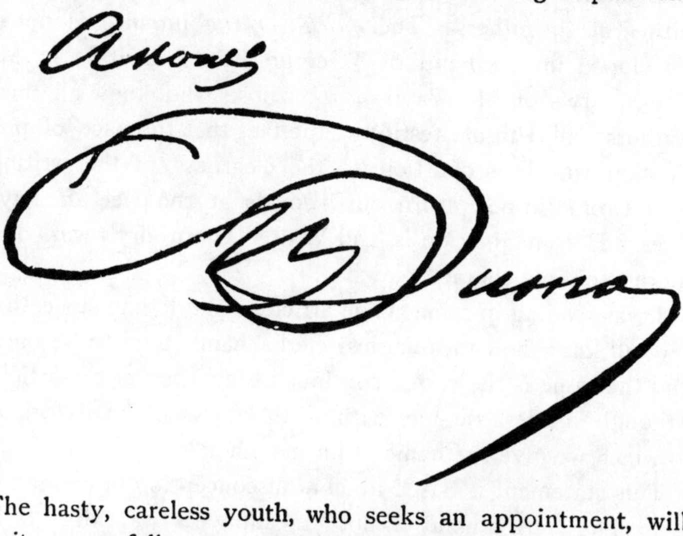

The hasty, careless youth, who seeks an appointment, will write a carefully prepared letter, and one may judge of him erroneously in consequence, unless care be exercised.

Many very clever men and women write very illegible hands. Their brains often hurry them away, imagination takes the bit between its teeth and gallops off. Hence, "bad" writing.

Do not let me be misunderstood. I do not mean to say that all imaginative authors or other individuals write more or less illegibly. What I mean is this—that imaginative writers, whose brains work very quickly and impulsively, always write very quickly, and as a consequence somewhat less intelligibly than the perhaps equally imaginative, but less impulsive energetic authors.

The late "George Eliot" and the late Mr. Thornbury, or the living Mr. James Payn, wrote (and write) with great imaginative power; but compare the first-named writing with either of the others. The *quick-working* impulse is not so developed in the hand of "George Eliot" as it is in Mr. Thornbury's or Mr. Payn's; and those who knew all these authors will, I think, testify to the fact that the pace of production was in proportion to the clearness of the writing. Mrs. Cross did not "turn out" novels at the pace Mr. Payn does. His imagination is, and Walter Thornbury's was, of a more excitable character.

I was reading in a magazine article, a short time since, that "we all know how meaningless clerks' hands tend to become; and the same is the case," continued the writer of the article, "though in a less degree, with all that class of handwritings to which we give the name of business hands."

This statement is based upon a misconception of handwriting. The clerk's hand is not "meaningless" at all! It is entirely characteristic of a clerk's neatness, order, love (or practice), of detail—mechanical to a certain extent, we admit. Is not a clerk a kind of machine in his office? The same test will apply to the business hand: clearness, love of detail, straightforwardness, absence of personality, self-contained coolness. Are not these business qualities? and would you not, then, rather expect a business man to write a plain, and which to some may appear a "meaningless" hand? Yet all the while the hand is the index to the man's character.

Apropos of clerks' writing, I was once tackled triumphantly by a critic, who wanted to know why, if the crossing of the letter *t* be a sign of will and assurance, determination and action, the handwriting of the average clerk showed a very mild crossing of the *t?* Surely the explanation is obvious. A clerk at work has virtually no will of his own. He copies, he obeys, he has no independent existence *qua* clerk; but put him to write a challenge to a cricket match or a football engagement, and I venture to think that you will find a little more force in the writing, and, where will is required, in the crossing of the *t*'s.

We may go even farther than this, and investigate the handwriting of a quick-witted, energetic, impulsive clerk. His penmanship will be more flowing, and divulge more rapidity of thought—it may be more carelessness—than the regular penmanship of the plodding individual. He is more imaginative. This is the man who, when his working hours are over, will entirely put aside "the shop," and go in for—or go out for—amusement, acting in private theatricals or such-like "fun." The man who will most likely succeed as a clerk is he who is to a certain extent devoid of imagination, and who will plod along carefully, not thinking overmuch for himself outside his duties. Your imaginative authors generally will not succeed as editors, for this same reason.

If any proof be required as to the influence of the mind on the handwriting, and the exposition of how the development of the will and independence alter the character of the writing, let us examine the penmanship of a number of lads who are taught by the same writing-master. It has been stated that boys form their hands on their master's, copy *him*, and *therefore* handwriting in these cases can be no indication of character.

Now the intelligent reader will at once perceive the futility of such an argument. Perhaps, so long as the lads are under the eyes and influence of the master they will copy his writing, because he for the time being dominates their minds and, maybe, forms their characters ; but as they grow older do not they change their writing ? Do not individual characteristics crop up and change the penmanship ? If the character did not alter, the person would write a childish hand ; candid, open, perhaps, but without signs of intelligence, of will, or of self: in fact, without any very definite characteristics.

Exception has been made in my hearing to Graphology, as being only applicable to our own national handwriting—that the English graphologist can only delineate the characters of his countrymen and countrywomen. I think this suggestion will be found to have no real basis. If one be acquainted with the French, German, Spanish, or other handwriting, and with the language, I opine that there would be no more difficulty in deciphering a character from a letter written in any of these languages than in reading an English character. So far as French goes, I am certain it can be done; and if so, why not in Italian and Spanish ? The writer above quoted says: "We are inclined to think that Frenchmen, Germans, Italians, and Spaniards almost all write very much alike." This is tantamount to saying that Germans, Frenchmen, Italians, and Spaniards have all about the same dispositions and characteristics—a contention obviously absurd. Why should the English character only be observable in handwriting? If it be discernible in English correspondence, as it certainly is, why not in the penmanship of Italians, which, by the way, is peculiarly graceful and artistic, as a rule; and the national character may be deduced from it.

It is also quite possible to tell the shape and appearance of the hand itself from the appearance of the handwriting. This can be easily proved, and some day it will be my care to bring this forward, and prove the intimate alliance which exists between the means and the production.

The invention of the present system of Graphology is attributed to M. l'Abbé Flandrin, of Paris. He imparted his system to several pupils, but, so far as I am aware has left no written rules behind him. But the energetic and ingenious Debarrolles, author of the "Mysteries of the Hand," and kindred works, has arranged the system with the assistance of one of the Abbé's pupils. To him our English writers are, in the first place, mainly indebted. But French writing is not for our learning. It differs in many respects. So we have studied for ourselves.

In these pages I have given the results of much observation and practice, and will now proceed to put down in order the general rules for the guidance of the student of Graphology.

We have a few more remarks to make as regards the writing of the sexes, and we may at once state that no particular style of handwriting is peculiar to either sex. There are many ladies who write like men, and many men who write a "ladylike" hand. It is impossible to tell, for certain, whether a letter is the production of a man or of a woman.

The fact that the penmanship of women has undergone a change during the last quarter of a century has furnished a text for some objections against our theories ; but when we consider that the occupations, the ideas, and the amusements of women very closely approximate to those of men, now-a-days, we cannot be surprised to find that their writing reflects something, and in some cases a great deal, of the masculine element. I am speaking now of the ordinary members of society, for I fancy that in all ages talent and imagination would have been found in the writing of authoresses, if they had been sought.

CHAPTER I.

I.—Of the Styles of Handwriting, and the Direction of the Lines Written.

ONE of the first things to learn in the study of Graphology is the cultivation of the art of reading without taking in the *sense* of the letter. I do not deny that at times an idea of the writer may be gained from his mode of expression; but then you do not act as you profess to act. You are not telling his character from his handwriting exclusively, if you are also studying his mood, as shown in his connected or disconnected sentences, his angry words or cool sarcasms. No; to delineate character you must try, at any rate, to be able to dispense with such aids to learning.

The capability will come by practice, and you will, after a while, be able to read a letter without in any way hurting the feelings of any one who may have feared to entrust you with the communication from his friend. Any breach of confidence will thus be avoided.

Having mastered this not very difficult lesson, the *appearance of the writing* is the next thing to consider. Is it *even*, or *ascending*, or *sloping downwards?* Each of the signs have a certain signification.

(1.) *If it be even*, the writer is in good health, calm, straightforward, determined; that is, knowing what he is about, firm. Want of firmness may arise from a tired hand,

and then the general signs must be investigated. But as a rule, we accept the even handwriting as an even, straightforward, candid character; honest and simple-minded in its regularity. (The details will be investigated presently, as we proceed.)

(2.) *If it be ascending*, ambition, energy, activity, perseverance and ardour, are all indicated. This is the reason why we frequently see successful men writing in an ascending style. Strong will is also indicated by the ascending writing; it is, in fact, the sign-manual of the persevering and ascending worker, he mounts higher and higher. No specimen is needed for our illustration. Any reader will recognise the truth of the description. Ardour, will, and position in society are frequently all indicated in the feminine ascending writing.

The ascending writing then may be called that of the "lucky" ones; but we must not forget that "luck," so-called, is most frequently the result of our own activity and energy.

(3.) *The descending writing* indicates melancholy, discouragement, timidity, weakness of health, and suffering. There is a want of will-power amongst the melancholy ones of the earth, and drooping spirits are indicated by drooping writing. I will illustrate this tendency by an anecdote, a true experience.

On a certain occasion, I received a letter from a lady, and in replying to it, I expressed my regret at perceiving her handwriting so sloping downwards, as I was afraid she was suffering, or would shortly suffer. I had no answer for awhile; then came a note commencing: "Oh, you fore-teller of evil!" The weakness indicated by the writing had come suddenly, unexpectedly, and had caused great suffering for some days. This attack had supervened almost immediately after the receipt of my letter. Other similar experiences might be narrated, but this one will suffice.

(4.) There is a fourth aspect in which the handwriting must be considered, and that is, when it appears both descending and ascending; the beginning tending upwards or running straight, and then falling away in its firmness. This appearance indicates a struggle of some kind, either against bodily weakness or against financial or other difficulties. The energy is there, but worry tends to drag it down. On the other hand, the writing may commence with a downward tendency, and the brain and will may struggle successfully against Fate for a time—yet we shall generally find that the activity is not sustained—the lines fall again. As we have said above, such writing means that a struggle, a fight, is going on against destiny or circumstances.

These four indications must be noted by the learner, and when he, or she, has mastered these little accomplishments, and, as it were, grasped the appearance of the writing as a whole, the details may be studied. Of these details we will now proceed to speak, and as in all Grammars the alphabet comes first, so in this book we will commence with the individual letters.

The letters in writing, it is unnecessary to add, occur as capitals and small letters, and at the commencement, middle, and terminations of words; initials and finals have certain significations attached to them. The initials have a peculiarity, inasmuch as the more harmonious their form, the more they resemble printed letters, the more poetic is the temperament of the writer.

We thus have a general rule, the more clear, well-formed

and simple the initial, the more poetic, simple and graceful are the temperament and taste. Intelligence and cultivation are presupposed, with sense of form and artistic taste if the letter be "in proportion," and of even, rounded, lines.

Another rule; when want of form and harmony are noticed, pretension and carelessness, ardour, eccentricity, etc., are present in the temperament. We will proceed to give some, examples by which the rules will be the more readily understood.

II.—Of the Letters; Initials and Others.

Some letters of the alphabet are much more expressive, and give one more insight into character than others. Perhaps the capital M and the terminal *e*, are the most telling of all. But many others, the C, the D, the L, N, and A are all of great use as initials, while the small *d* is a wonderful touchstone for vanity and imagination.

If we were to give examples of all the letters of the alphabet, this section would occupy too much space. We will content ourselves, therefore, with some general rules and examples, by means of which the reader will readily understand all the letters, and which he may apply to all in turn. The same test of common sense may be used in all these instances.

We annex in the margin two samples of capital A's. The former, you see, is plain, clear, unpretentious, without flourish or swagger. Now, applying your common-sense, O reader! to those two examples, which would, you think, indicate the nicer disposition?

(1.) The clear elegant capital, which bears some resemblance to a type letter, is what is termed "harmonious;" the firm, quickly-made bar indicates *firmness* and *vivacity;* the approach to type-form *poetry;* and the graceful elegant form, grace and elegance. The nearer this letter—or any other—approaches type clearness and shape the more poetic is the temperament.

(2.) This initial A is sprawling; there is no sense of harmony in it; there is excitability, and a somewhat ill-regulated imagination.

A man who would flourish his writing like this would have little moral courage, and a good deal of self-appreciation and pretension.

As regards the small *a*'s (and the same rule applies to the small *o*'s), we shall find that like people's mouths some are habitually closed and some open. These letters indicate exactly the tendencies of the writers, just as surely as the closed mouth gives us the idea of caution and discretion, and the open lips the chattering, garrulous person. As a matter of fact, the *a* closed indicates in Graphology a cautious, self-contained person, who will not "wear his heart upon his sleeve." The open *a* or *o* points to the contrary, a talkative person, a gossip. There are modifications, of course; these are the rules.

A well-made capital A, is a sign of intelligence. An open small *a*, is a sign of chattiness; a closed small *a* is a sign of caution and reserve. A badly made capital A, is imaginative, eccentric, pretentious, and narrow-minded, in proportion.

In the same manner, we come to a conclusion respecting our B's. The well-made gracefully rounded B is a type of good taste, poetic temperament, a cultivated mind. Of course, it will degenerate

into eccentricity, self-complacency, extravagance, pretension according as it is less clear and elegant, and more "flourishy." The initial on p. 21 cannot be said to indicate any sense of beauty or harmony. The second specimen, on the contrary, is graceful, and indicates a critical and cultivated mind. As regards small *b*'s, there is not much to indicate. Looped, they show in common with all looped letters, affection and kind-heartedness, but have no special signification. They are not a type.

The letter C gives us a considerable insight into character, inasmuch as it is capable of many diverse forms, and in some hands becomes ostentatious or vulgar; and, again, is capable of great artistic expression. The soft round curve tells us of the gentle, *dolce far niente* nature. The large and far-extending C tells us of great ardour and imagination. We append three examples, two indicating the harmony, the other the discord of Graphology. The last is too unbounded in its flourishes. The letter is very neat. There is nothing specially to be learnt from the small *c*. The rules as to other letters will apply to it. C, with a curly tail, is egotistic.

D is another useful letter, and its forms are numerous. The small *d*, in particular, is most important, and no student of Graphology will neglect to study its varied, and modified, or exaggerated forms. As regards the capital D, the usual rule obtains. The rounded clear and neat letter speaks for itself. The small *d* is herewith shown in two somewhat exaggerated specimens. The small back curve of the *d* indicates imagination, but too much curl is vanity, self-sufficiency; the more inharmonic the form the more foolish the pretension.

The first specimen underneath, the reader will immediately recognise as indicating presumption, and self-appreciation. The specimen can be compared with others. The second specimen is ill-regulated imagination, unbounded

almost, and ridiculous oftentimes; want of "harmony." But when the small *d* is united to the letter immediately following, it indicates a well-regulated mind, a sequence in ideas. The curve without the extravagant flourish is good.

The letter E, in the capital form, is not very important. It gives us some insight into character in its curves; firmness, elegance and taste, may by it be recognised. The curl back in the E, when the tail is thrown back, as in the C, turning over from right to left, indicates some selfishness.

The small *e* is a very characteristic letter. In its Greek form is shown cultivation, education. In its long elevated "tail," generosity, imagination, ardour, and indeed carelessness of life, if too long and thick. The following specimen will indicate this tendency. It is from the pen of the brave General Cambronne, to whom has been attributed the fiction concerning the non-surrender of the battalion of the Imperial Guard at Waterloo.

We may pass quickly by the letters F, G, H, I, J, K, and L. The last is, perhaps, the most suitable for study; but all those letters must be judged by the fundamental rules of distinctness and elegance of form, flourish, and firmness, which have already been explained. The nearer they approach to type form, the more poetic instinct they reveal, and with a little flourish show imagination.

Here are two letters, one from the pen of a gallant soldier, the other from that of a poet. No one can mistake which is which. The poetic and critical faculty, with imagination, are developed in the word "George."

We can dismiss I, J, K, and L without any further discussion, and come directly to the letter of most importance, M. We have in this letter such a variety of shapes, sometimes written with two upstrokes, sometimes with three; sometimes these strokes are all equal; sometimes one is highest, and all different in height, curves, turns, and many varieties of them.

Thus M attains an important place. Pride in the first stroke is frequently seen, accuracy, attainment of one's ambition, a struggling after the unattainable, want of brain power—all these characteristics are observable in letter

We can give examples, which may be compared with letters of individuals known to the reader. These forms are merely specimens written by the author himself, though actual excerpts could be doubtless found.

The first indication in the M may be pride. This is exhibited by the high first stroke, in which pride, ambition, and a desire to win may be seen. A person writing such a letter will have not attained his ideal in life

But a man may have reached his goal in life or nearly so. Then we shall find him writing a different M. He will equalize the upstrokes, and in the clearness and simplicity of his letters will show precision, neatness, reflection, and so on.

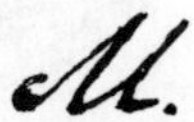

A person who puts a high flourish to the terminal of the M is cursed with an imagination to which his judgment will eventually succumb. The curve also indicates some vanity, but the formation is by no means bad, apart from the flourish, which, if smaller, will modify the censure it implies. For instance, here is another specimen given to illustrate meanings. In this instance it will be observed that the second limb of the letter rises high above the other. Here is force of character displayed. The curve shows egoism in a small degree. Such a letter as this indicates an ideal sought but not attained. Such an one as the following denotes the attainment of ambition or position in life—a kind of satisfied longing. The strokes are nearly equal in height.

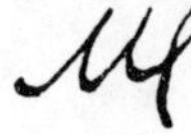

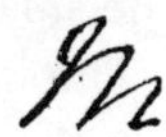

There are almost infinite varieties of M's, from the clear, simple forcible initial of Father Hyacinthe to the vulgar scrawl of a communist. We might multiply examples, but the reader will readily adapt these rules to his sense of perception.

Letter N can be judged by the same rules. Here is one specimen of an N which is more like the eagle than the N in appearance. It is another specimen of

Cambronne's caligraphy, and in which great eccentricity would readily be found by any reader.

The subsequent letters, O, P, Q, R, S, although they lend themselves to interpretation, are not of very serious import beyond the ordinary line of criticism, and usual rules. But T, and particularly in the small letter, is very important. The small *t* is as characteristic as the capital M.

The importance of the *t* may be estimated from the fact that the crossing or barring indicates the writer's strength of will, his energy, his obstinacy, his weakness, his temper! All these signs are plainly to be seen in the small *t*, which we shall now consider.

The will of the individual is very clearly indicated by the strength and thickness of the bar, its length and its termination. Strong will is shown thus, energy is also indicated, and perseverance. A thick bar, firmly put down; its upper end hints at quick temper.

A dyspeptic person will cross his *t*'s high and firmly; a vivacious, quick person, will also cross them high, but the bar will "tail off," and not end in a hard, firm stop as if the end had been amputated. The *t* with only a

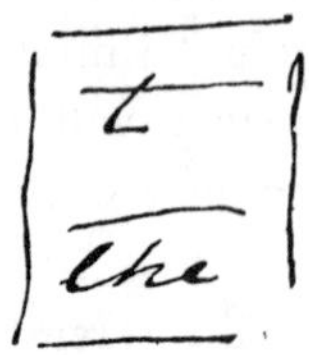

firm upstroke will also denote firmness, while a light bar will denote weak will and want of energy. Energy is shown in long bars. Numerous instances could be given, but illustration is quite unnecessary. The simple rule is very easily remembered, and tallies with our own experience. When we come to analysis of handwriting, and show specimens of correspondence, the traits will be observed.

The remainder of the alphabet need not be dissected. There are no unusual points observable in them. They follow the general rules, and may be judged by their clearness, etc., as B, C, and D. The Finals now claim our attention, briefly.

III.—The Terminals.

Having devoted some time to the capitals and intermediate letters, we will conclude this chapter with a few hints regarding the "terminals"; that is, the term used for those forms which end words—"Finals," some call them. Letters, we all know, assume different shapes in different hands—often in the same hand—so some explanation of their meaning is necessary. The following general rules may be accepted.

When letters appear suddenly to cease and terminate without any more expenditure of ink than is absolutely necessary to form them, or when they are hardly formed and cut short, we may fairly suppose that economy, and, perhaps, avarice is present in the character. The economy may be the result of circumstances, not from natural taste: so the space between the lines, the size of the writing, and such landmarks must be also noted.

An individual who writes a small, mean, close, sparing

hand, and docks his letters' tails too, may be regarded as miserly in his nature. But when we find space between lines and words, and plenty of paper used in writing and the words "docked," we must look to find reasons for economy, and will judge that the writer, with somewhat grand ideas, has been obliged to cultivate it. The small writing, when free from blemish, only means application to detail—a critical mind also—of this we shall treat later on.

When the final letters curve upwards we have at once indications of generosity, and when the writing is large, and extravagant in the use of pen and ink, we can convict the individual of, at least, a wish to have everything on a grand scale—his tastes are in that direction, and the spending of money would not be considered a fault in his eyes. A wide spreading hand, with curving finals, may be thus interpreted.

The unrestrained ease and dash of the uprising final is the consequence of a similar nature.

When words end in a somewhat angular manner and rise up, we have the indications of a tenacious temperament, mixed with elements of vivacity and quickness; but the angularity means quick temper and obstinacy, *l'homme têtu*. The other letters must be studied, of course.

The ascending final also tells of ambition; and gently rounded moulded terminals are considered types of elegance and artistic taste. But "many-angled terminations," as if the pen had been inclined to break up the words generally, indicate a roughness of temper, a want of cultivation, and an absence of the artistic taste.

Thus we perceive that roundness means ease; angularity, vivacity; an upward tendency, ambition and quick temper. Economy in ink is the sign-type of economy of temperament;

and liberality in penmanship-spacing, a tendency to extravagance in habit. The mind acts upon the hand, as is only natural, and the mental bias is reproduced in the writing.

We will now endeavour to give some illustrations and explanations of the various characteristics of human nature as indicated and expressed by writing. In necessary cases we will append specimens of writing, both English and French, and show how both languages can be interpreted with equal facility by the student of Graphology.

CHAPTER II.

Characteristics Apparent in Handwriting.

I.

ALL, or nearly all the passions, affections, and weaknesses of human nature may be discovered from the handwriting. This may appear a very bold statement to advance; but I venture to say, that before this book is ended the assertion will have been justified. The possibility acknowledged, it remains for the writer to show how the fact is accomplished.

It will be convenient to proceed in alphabetical order with our list; and I will here state that I do not intend to advance any statements which I have not personally verified, and have not by true experience tested. There are many very expert graphologists, and they will all testify to the feasibility of the delineations, and the general accuracy of the verdicts obtainable from penmanship. Now for our list of human characteristics :—

Affection, Ambition, Anger, Ardour, Artistic-taste, Avarice, Audacity.

Benevolence, Bashfulness, Brutality, Business-habits.

Calmness, Candour, Caution, Coarseness, Coldness, Conscientiousness, Criticism, Cruelty, Cultivation.

Deceit, Despotism, Detail, Despondency, Determination, Deductiveness, Diplomacy, Dissimulation.

Eccentricity, Economy, Egotism, Enthusiasm, Eloquence, Energy, Extravagance, Excitability.

Falsehood, Facility, Fatality, Finesse, Firmness, Ferocity, Flattery, Frankness.

Generosity, Gentleness, Grandeur.

Honesty, Honour, Humility, Hypocrisy, Heroism.

Ill-Health, Indecision, Imagination, Impulse, In, dolence, Intelligence, Impatience.

Jealousy, Judgment, Jocosity.

Kindness.

Laziness, Logic, Love, Lucidity of mind.

Magnificence, Melancholy, Minutiæ, Modesty, Mathematical Mind, Music.

Nobility of Mind, Neatness.

Obstinacy, Order, Originality.

Parsimony, Penetration, Patience and Perseverance, Poetic Feeling, Pride, Prodigality.

Quickness of Thought, Quarrelsomeness.

Refinement, Reserve.

Selfishness, Self-Sufficiency, Self-Devotion, Self-Containedness, Scientific Taste, Sensitiveness, Sensuality, Sensuousness, Simplicity, Sincerity, Spontaneity, Superiority, Struggle in Life.

Tact, Temper, Tenacity, Tenderness, Thrift, Truthfulness, Untruthfulness.

Vanity, Versatility, Vivacity, Vulgarity.

Will, in various degrees, Want of Will, Weakness, Worry.

II.

We may accept the foregoing list as a fairly representative one. There are modifications of many characteristics, which will subsequently be explained in our chapter on Contradictory Symptoms and on Contrasts. We will now proceed to discuss the first type of character, an universal one, viz., Affection, Affectionateness.

AFFECTION, that is fondness, and a power of loving, can be determined almost at a glance in any handwriting. Its best characteristics are long loops to the letters, with a rather sloping hand. The letters are tenderly formed, if one may so speak; and the y's frequently turn back instead of rounding to the left, thereby giving generosity of affection. Frequently, rounded letters will be seen, in a rather upright hand. This is a modification of affection; a somewhat harder and more selfish type. Again, when the writing is thick, rounded, and sloping, and also embellished with long loops, we have passionate affection; regard for the opposite sex.

There are, therefore, degrees in the writing as in the temperament. In the specimens annexed the difference in the expression of affection will be seen in two cases. The former is much more sentimental, and perhaps, more sensitive than the other. We say "perhaps more sensitive," because the self-control and reserve of the latter writer would not *show* the feeling so much, but we believe the wound would be there. The former is more generally affectionate in her disposition than the latter; the latter is much less given to the "wearing of the heart upon the sleeve." Both indicate delicacy of mind, and some sentimentalism.

AMBITION is ascertainable from an energetic and upward sloping handwriting. We mean a writing in which the general character of the words as well as of the lines is ascendant. The same signification may be attached to the final letters.

But Ambition without Will, or, in default of Will, Diplomacy, is null and void. Strong determination will perhaps succeed in the long run; but *finesse*, tact, and diplomacy, will do more than steady, plodding perseverance.

There are numerous instances which will occur to readers who have only to look at the handwriting of any one whom they know is pushing and ambitious. The student will then perceive the same characteristics, and may argue by analogy concerning other types. These illustrations will bear investigation.

ANGER will be found, as common-sense will have already determined, in a very *quick movement* of the pen. The first thing to look for in the writing of people easily irritated is the crossing of the *t*. If the *t* is barred high, and in a "fly-away" manner, particularly when the bar is firm and thick, you may be certain that the writer is a touchy, irritable person, and of a rather sulky temperament too. The obstinacy will give tenacity; and tenacity in anger may be termed "sulks." The high, quick bar and angular writing will tell of Anger, quick, and perhaps fierce, and the varying heights of the letters will indicate a *want of calmness* and self-restraint. Hence anger, and often restlessness, irritability, and, when the individual is thwarted, bad temper, arise. We need not give an illustration, though we could do so. It would be invidious to pillory an acquaintance in this manner Ascending bars to the *t*'s, angular writing, and the indications of *energy* and *vivacity*, will generally give us a quick-tempered person, particularly if obstinacy be present.

ARDOUR is represented in Graphology in much the same manner as Energy. The soaring indication of the letters, the curved finals, and such signs of ardour and even of "exaggerated enthusiasm" if the capitals be too big and the flourishes exuberant. The ardour of an enthusiastic person will be visible in the elongated capitals, and the firm sweep of the letters; in the long flying bars to *t*'s and the general "go" in the writing.

There are ardour, enthusiasm, and many other serviceable qualities in the accompanying specimen, with *finesse*.

We now come to a rather more complex characteristic: namely, Artistic taste, which is to a certain extent allied to poetic feeling and refinement. Principally you will discover this, the artistic indication, in the clearness and the gracefulness of the capitals. If we superadd imagination we have most of the qualities of the artist. But artistic taste may, and very frequently does, exist without any of the

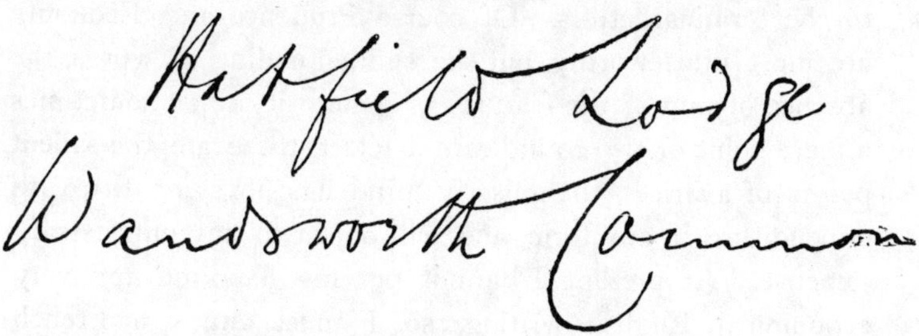

power of execution. People who have a taste for sculpture and love for architecture generally make their capitals of a print-like accuracy, without the same signs of imagination as distinguished the painter, or the lover of painting. The characteristics are more severe in tone; but, of course, sculptors have imagination strongly developed unless they are mere copyists.

The elegant, rounded, capital letter is thus indicative of artistic taste in painting; the more severe form is more allied to the architectural in art. With imagination and a somewhat thick writing, it shows a leaning to the *poetic* side. But "artistic taste," as a whole, may be deduced from the artistic capitals; the perception of form, and the harmony of proportion.

AVARICE, a very evident, but a somewhat unpleasant characteristic is the next on the list. The tendencies of an avaricious nature are patent to every one. We have economy carried to an extraordinary extent, and a general desire to be sparing in all things.

Once more the common-sense side of Graphology is presented to us. The stingy, avaricious person will write a stingy hand, frequently small, and cramped, and close; sparing of ink and paper; no generous curves and flourishes to the terminal letters. Of course Prudence and Economy are most praiseworthy, but the sudden ending of words, the absence of any of the features of generosity (*q.v.*) sometimes a mere point or two to indicate a letter, these are the salient points of avarice; the miserly mind has no sympathy with expenditure in any form, and will object to any unnecessary expense. At present I cannot put my hand on any very economical English writing, so I must annex a French specimen, which will do equally well.

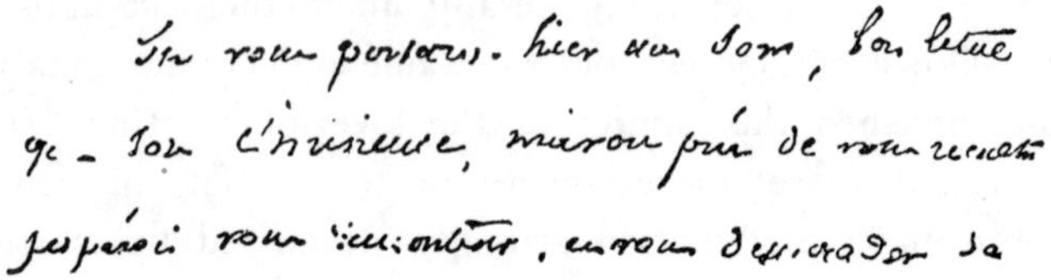

There is, nevertheless, an economy of prudence and praiseworthy dislike to extravagance which is very commonly seen. The few words we feel justified in annexing will illustrate our meaning. In the accompanying sentence, there is no meanness, no petty saving. The wide spaces show a liberal tone of mind, but good housekeeping would result if the lady whose writing is here shown, were placed in charge of her parent's household.

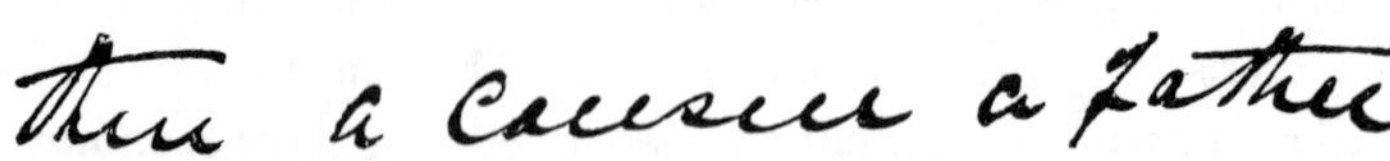

In this writing you see, or will see, when you have studied Graphology, a very charming, kind disposition. Witness the *n* and *u*, and the clear but not extravagant endings of the first three words. Here is all the difference.

In the first specimen, the writing was close and cramped, here is the generous instinct restrained by prudence and principle. There is great firmness, self-control, and decision of character in this writing.

Frequently we find a miserly person spending money liberally. This will be the case when his ideas of enjoyment are selfish, and he wishes to please himself or gain some advantage. We have ourselves been the guest of a man to whose table we were verbally invited with a friend. Everything was well done, and our elderly host, a charming man, did all he could to please and tempt our palates. But soon afterwards a reason became apparent—a favour was suggested, but skilfully veiled. In a letter of thanks for compliance with the request preferred, the economy (rather the stinginess and closeness) of the person came out, and we perceived the selfish trait plainly enough. But had we never seen the handwriting, the real character which we have since verified would have remained concealed. The man was rich, and liked to do things grandly in public, but in ordinary circumstances he was mean in the extreme.

If the reader will refer to the paragraphs upon generosity and prodigality, he will, by comparison with the writing of his own acquaintances, quickly discover with what wonderful correctness the deductions from handwriting can be made.

We must again warn the reader that there are in every handwriting many contradictions, and he must not condemn Graphology because it tells him the truth. The individual may *appear* to be liberal, honourable, truthful; and yet his unstudied hand, that is, his natural writing, may reveal baseness and dissimulation! There may also be modifications: practice and attention to details will very soon teach the learner discrimination, and he will distinguish the various shades correctly and well.

III.—Of Bashfulness, Benevolence, Business.

We must now proceed to the next letter, B.

The first trait, in alphabetical order, is BASHFULNESS, which may be described as a combination of shyness and modesty. The natural humility which we must look for is indicated in writing, by the close fitting strokes of capital letters, and the small letters even, moderate, and not showy. The M, the N, and such letters; perhaps, also A, may be studied for shyness and humility, and with the rather small writing will be decisive of bashfulness and moderation in taste and habits.

Your grandee, or the men of great self-assertion, will write a big showy hand, and space out his capitals. Your modest and retiring correspondent, on the contrary, will be modest and self-contained. There is no possibility of error. Look at the following handwriting, and say whether you

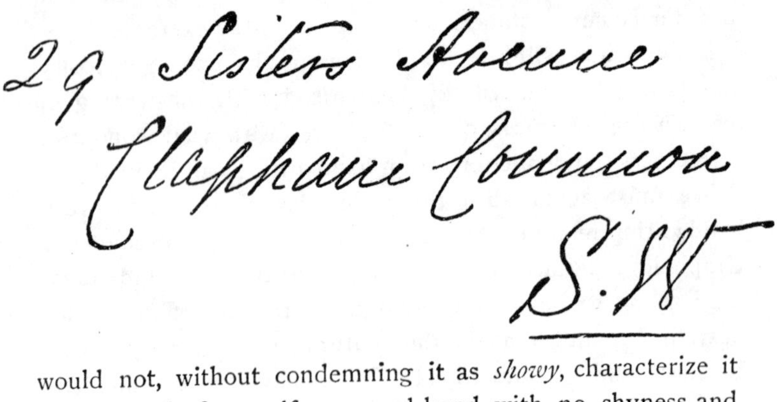

would not, without condemning it as *showy*, characterize it as a *masterly*, firm self-possessed hand, with no shyness and bashfulness in its well-formed large letters, its kindness, and liveliness, and economy in details. There are other points, but we need not particularise them now.

BENEVOLENCE is discovered in the character by the openness and clearness of the writing: there is no violence in it; but there is activity displayed, with clear candid letters, and a truthful, open nature. There was not much difficulty in deducing the characteristics from such a hand as we annex below, which, nevertheless, combines frankness with caution, liberality without extravagance, affection without strong passion. The writing is not a perfect specimen of benevolence, but will serve for our illustration.

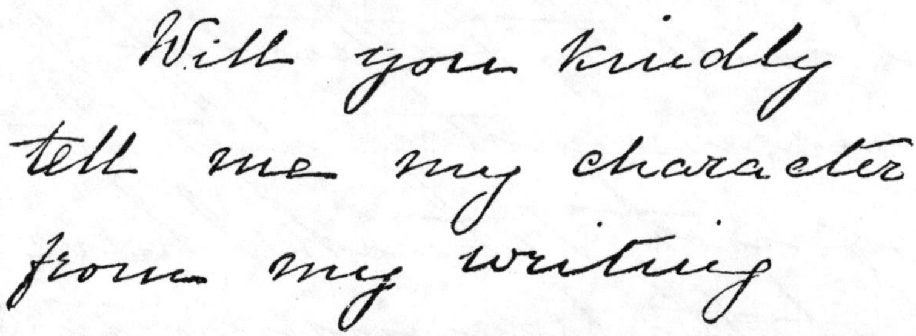

The characteristics of a benevolent person are, then, largeness of mind in even writing, flowing, graceful, terminations to the letters which slope. In really benevolent writing there is a total absence of flourish in the large, candid, caligraphy; some will-power and affection.

BRUTALITY is a trait not often discerned, at least not in our own experience of handwriting. It is sometimes seen even in the writing of more or less educated people, and allied to ferocity and sensuality; a thick heavy writing with little intelligence in it; impulsive, with strongly barred *t*'s, ungraceful withal—may be classed as of the brutal nature.

Force and will are the principal characteristics, with a want of cultivation. (See CRUELTY, COARSENESS, and SENSUALITY.)

BUSINESS habits are generally recognised by a neat, cautious, well-punctuated writing, in which abbreviations sometimes occur. A methodical writing, an orderliness, is observable throughout, and the stops carefully inserted, *i*'s dotted, and *t*'s carefully crossed. This is the plodding, careful, persevering, "business" hand, without much imagination. The same general character with more energy, will, and *dash* in it, will be observable in the writing of those who decide

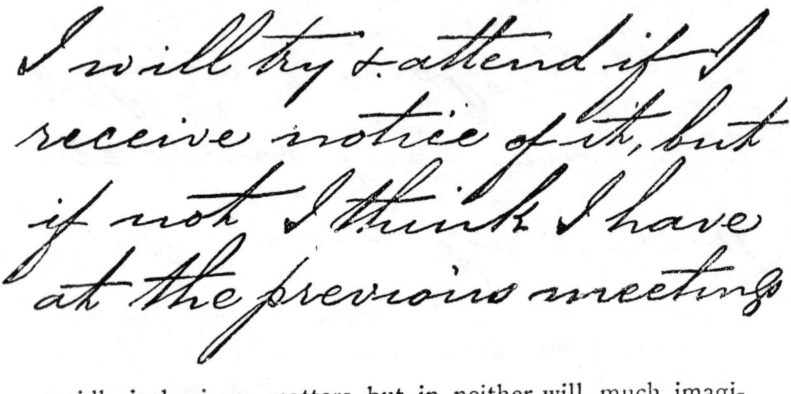

rapidly in business matters, but in neither will much imagination be visible.

Here is a most persevering business hand, a kind-hearted specimen, with plenty of energy and movement, care and caution in dots and stops. Very fair in his dealings we should say; candid, but not a man to be imposed upon for all his good nature.

IV.—Of Calmness, Candour, Caution, Criticism, Cruelty, and Cultivation.

Calmness and Candour may be seen in the two accompanying specimens. The calmness is perceptible in the even sizes of the letters, if they were of different sizes *versatility* would be indicated, or restlessness. The conspicuous candour of the second specimen is easily perceived.

Candour being seen in the open lines and sloping letters, if the words are separated evenly also, there is no mistake possible. The former specimen is closer, rather self-contained, with considerable tenacity in the crossing of the *t*'s, but frankness and truthfulness are equally apparent.

Caution can be discerned in the business

hand. A tendency to put in the stops after numbers and names ; a careful tone, the pauses and crosses all regular. The careful address with stops after initials will also indicate caution.

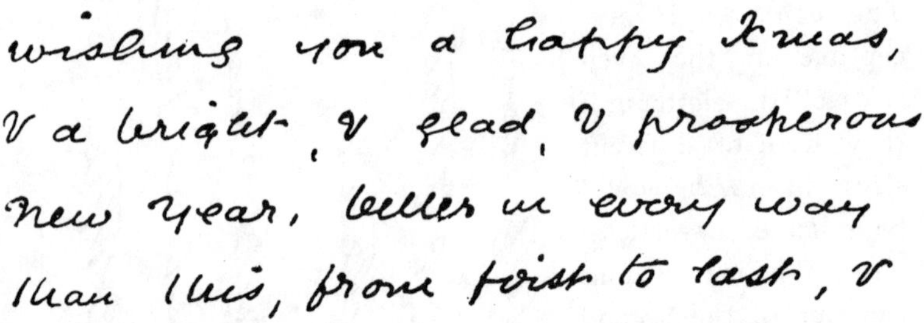
wishing you a happy Xmas, & a bright, & glad, & prosperous New Year, better in every way than this, from first to last, &

Here is considerable caution. See the stops and the dotting of the *i*'s, which also betoken orderliness ; this is not a demonstrative hand.

COARSENESS we need not dwell upon. The thick, blunt, perhaps clever, writing, of a sensual character will be a sign-post. There is a want of refinement and elegance in such penmanship. We have no specimen of coarseness to exhibit, the general characteristics will be easily understood.

COLDNESS of heart is generally seen in the handwriting of the selfish people. We mean the coldness which is want of sympathy, not the absence of passion, for many cold-hearted people have plenty of passion of a sensual kind, and yet are unsympathetic in ordinary affairs and occasions.

These people usually write upright hands, without any generous flowing curves and capitals. The letters are generally closed up, showing self-containedness ; and if the writing be rather thin, there is little love wasted on any one. If the writing is thick, there is self-indulgence, and a tendency to "animalism." There is no sloping tenderness, and no long loops—the writing is generally small also. If large, upright, and heavy, and "close," you will find the individual chatty,

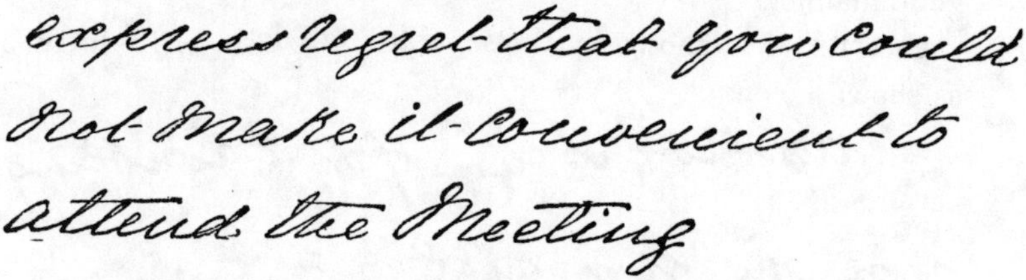

fond of admiration from the opposite sex, but very careful in responding—while permitting flirtation never committing herself or himself. The heart is not on the sleeve. We have seen several hands of this character, and have never been wrong in our estimation of the writers. Of course, there are degrees, and the other better signs may, and frequently do, modify the bad ones.

CONSCIENTIOUS people write steady, even hands, with a firm decided pen. The instance we gave just now of calm-

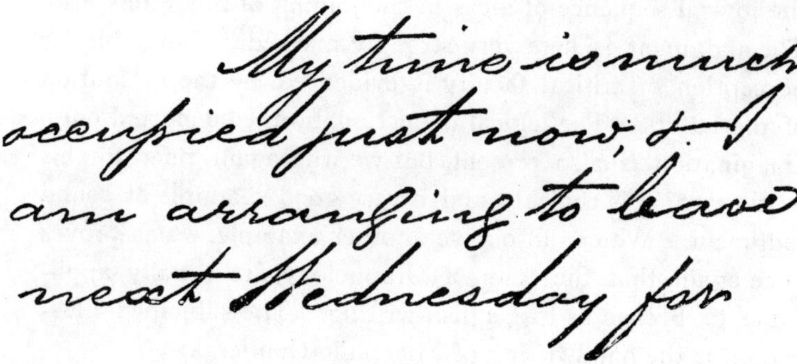

ness is a striking illustration of a conscientious person. The equality of spaces between lines argues a sense of justice;

neatness means clearness—nothing to conceal—a true honest temperament. This fragment from a business letter already annexed, will also show the same signs, but in a more energetic manner.

CRITICISM is shown by the separation of letters in a word as shown below.

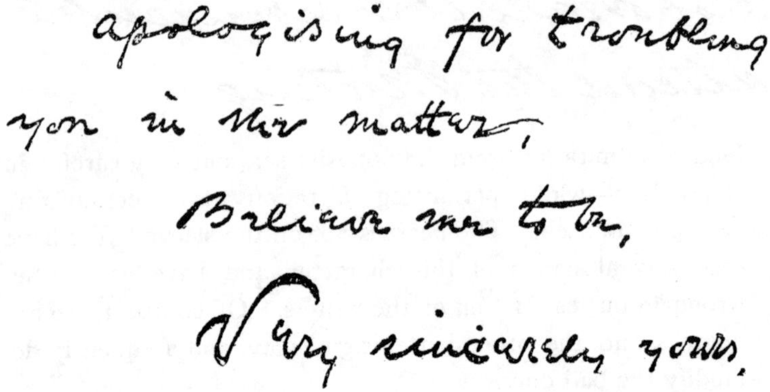

There is both the critical and the deductive faculty in the above writing. We have the separation of the letters, and the logical sequence of ideas in the joining of the letters also. The judgment is here very strongly marked. The inductive perception or critical faculty is evidenced by the separation of the letters. The logical deduction by the connected ones. Imagination is also present, but we will again refer to this writing which is typical—and a very good example of sound judgment. We can also give another example, which proves once again that the laws of Graphology are equally applicable to French as to English writing. The subjoined illustration is the handwriting of Theophile Gautier.

[OBSERVATION is denoted by the separation of the letters, the long and somewhat eccentric flourish indicates originality.]

Two principal tests are thus applied to the writings of critics, each of which denotes a different and almost contrary faculty; the power of discriminating, and the power of connecting incidents. All good critics possess these, and they give judgment.

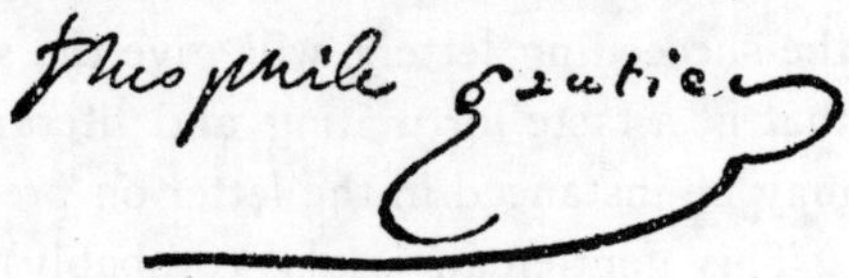

CRUELTY, like coarseness, may be quickly dismissed. It is evidenced in a thick writing. Anger is indicated by the thickly barred *t*'s, while the more selfishly upright writing shows want of consideration for others. If cruelty is quick, hurried, persevering, and hasty, we find a fierce individual. (See FEROCITY.)

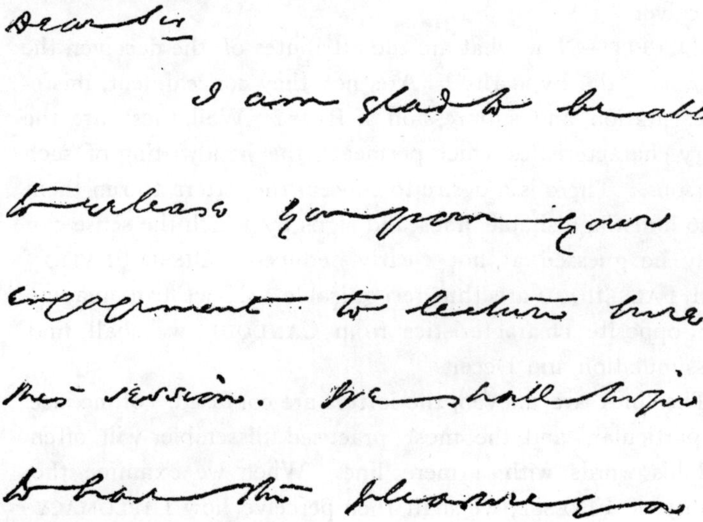
Dear Sir

I am glad to be able to release you from your engagement to lecture here this session. We shall hope to have the pleasure of a visit next session.

CULTIVATION is evidenced by rather small writing. The words, especially the small *d's*, being looped, and united with the succeeding letters, will give the signs of literary tastes—that is, a taste for writing and literary work. The *pressman* may be instanced in the letter on preceding page.

This gentleman is also (probably) a good speaker as well as a journalist. His ideas, we see, are logical, and his pen runs easily along the paper. There are many other good points (judgment, for instance) in this hand.

V.—OF DECEIT, DIPLOMACY, DISSIMULATION, DETAIL, AND DESPONDENCY.

We have considered Candour and Conscientiousness; let us, as a contrast, now examine the handwriting of the deceiver.

DECEIT.—Now what are the attributes of the deceiver, the liar, and the hypocrite? Are not they concealment, misrepresentation, and suppression of facts? Well, these are the very characteristics which permeate the handwriting of such persons. There is a desire to conceal the letters, to run them into indistinguishable lines and signs by which the sense can only be guessed at, not clearly deduced. DISSIMULATION and FALSEHOOD are thus recognisable. If we can imagine the opposite characteristics from CANDOUR, we shall find Dissimulation and Deceit.

The lines are uneven, the letters are confused, "of no size in particular," and the most practised dissembler will often end his words with a mere line. When we examine the quality of FINESSE, we shall then perceive how DIPLOMACY which is a recognised profession, may affect the handwriting. Seldom does an individual of very diplomatic mind write distinctly. He conceals his thoughts, his mind has cultivated the habit of concealment, and he will write as Talleyrand did —"diplomatically."

DIPLOMACY may be illustrated by an undulating and wary manner of writing, distinct enough, no doubt, but the *tendency* to conceal is there. The wavy line is very noticeable in the signature of Talleyrand, and in the line written by Count Cavour, which are annexed. These great diplomatists were of different characters, but their undulating writing betrayed the dominating diplomatic spirit. There is more ambitious

force in Cavour's hand, and a spark of enthusiasm. In the signature of Talleyrand is decadence—fatality! weakness of age, probably, not of intellect. Economy is very decided.

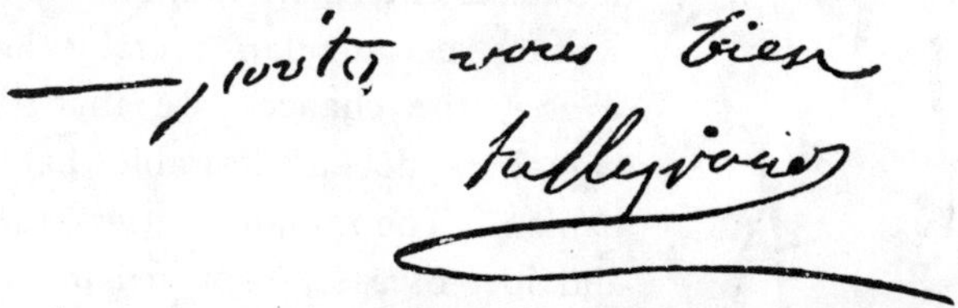

The reader must not confuse the haste of imaginative writing with the caligraphy of deceit. Frequently writers of vivid imagination are difficult to decipher, but this obscurity of writing is evidence of haste, not of deceit. The letters are generally all there, but not carefully formed. The hand endeavours to overtake the imagination, and an indistinct writing is the result. (See IMAGINATION, *sequel.*)

Many of the same indications of talent, *finesse,* obstinacy energy, and diplomacy, will be seen in the handwriting of Mr. Gladstone. His iron Will is very perceptible in the facsimile given later on; see also remarks on FINESSE. Ambition and self-esteem are also visible in the writing.

We have disposed of Deceit, Dissimulation, and Diplomacy in the foregoing paragraphs, as the qualities have somewhat parallel attributes; but, of course, care must be taken not to confound the deceiver with the politician. We can now pass on to Despotism, which makes itself apparent in the firm thick crushed down crossbar to the small *t*.

There is nothing more characteristic in Graphology than the crossing of the *t*. The Despot, the person (male or female) who crushes down the bar upon the letters, is extremely despotic; and if the writing be angular, thereby indicating *temper*, the chances are that the individual is not a desirable home companion. The rounded letters, the curves, and love of ease, displayed in some *pen-womanship*, will modify the signs, but a firm despotic character will always bar the *t*'s strongly. Here are some specimens; the reader's own experience will correct the writer if the latter err; but the reader will find it true, we venture to say, that despotic Will is evidenced in the *t*'s.

The above are instances of despotivity that is evident at a glance. The tremendous force is seen in the crushing crossing of the letters.

DETAIL.—The love of detail is firmly planted in some natures, and displays itself in small neat writing, in which every dot and dash is carefully put in, and the writing is rather upright. There does not appear to be much energy in such writing, the mind is too careful to run riot. The hand is well trained. So you can judge of an author or compiler who pays much attention to detail in the general rigidity of his handwriting. A man of imagination will betray himself even in compilation ; but your plodding, careful man of detail will write small and neatly, and with an upright pen. Publishers can thus choose their men at once. The writing below gives us a considerable attention to detail, which is naturally allied with carefulness, and caution, and affection.

"Where There's a will There's a way,
To seek it never give over,
For Though you mayn't find it Today
Tomorrow you may it discover."

Frequently the writing of those fond of detail is much smaller, and without the poetic taste exhibited in the foregoing lines. The love of detail will often impel people to underline an address, and put on the envelope not only "Clapton, N." (let us say), but Clapton, N., and *London* underlined in the corner of the envelope; or Twickenham, and *Middlesex* underlined in the opposite corner, just as we have seen the address of a letter to Paris, and *Seine* added, underlined, as if Paris was not sufficient address.

DESPONDENCY is one of the most easily recognisable traits

in Graphology. A weak desponding person, or one in ill-health, who is temporarily out of spirits, and therefore lacking in energy, will permit the hand to fall, the writing will slope downwards. A good deal might be written in this connection, and some apparent contradictions explained, but as the varied aspects of writing have been touched upon in Chapter I., we need only give an example, and to this example there hangs a tale, or rather a truth, which I will relate.

Some time ago the writer of the letter, a few lines of which are annexed, wrote to invite me to dinner. I replied, and in course of the note, regretted to be obliged to condole with her on physical weakness, because her somewhat sloping writing indicated approaching weakness and lassitude. For a few days no reply came, and then the letter arrived. It begins--

Oh! You foreteller of ill!!!

and goes on after a while, thus—

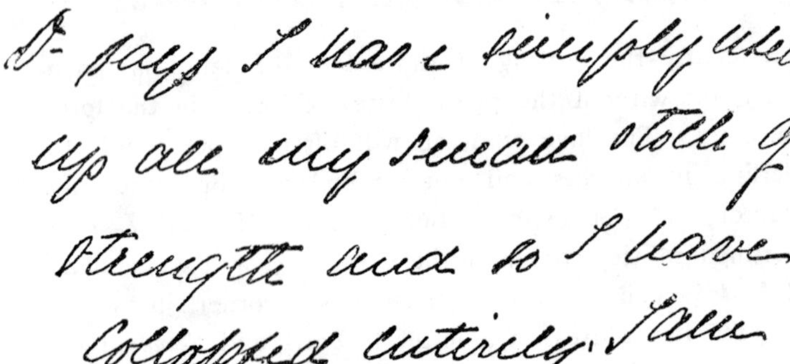
I- says I have simply used up all my small stock of strength and so I have collapsed entirely. Iam

Now here the reader may see a positive proof of the weakness foretold, which came to pass. I am glad to say that the temporary lassitude has long since passed away, and the writing is now stronger and more rigid in its lines. But the sloping and somewhat desponding tendency of the specimens will be apparent. It is surprising to people who have no knowledge of Graphology, to be informed that they themselves or their friend, whose writing is being dissected, is ailing or is haunted, often unknown to themselves, by a fatal weakness which is displayed in the ever-drooping hand. The malady may remain dormant for years, but the germ of *fatality* is in the writing—and dragging it down. Such writing may mean failure in life. The one thing needful is missed.

DETERMINATION can readily be recognised by the firm ness of the writing, and the steady crossing of the *t*. There is no need to enter into further explanation which would be more or less a repetition of the explanations of DESPOTISM, and WILL, and OBSTINACY. A straight firm bar to all the small *t*'s will indicate to us that the writer is determined. If the bar be rather "fly away," we have energy and quick temper as well. (See PERSEVERANCE.)

DEDUCTIVENESS is a quality allied to Criticism and Judgment. Intuitiveness of perception, and the deduction of a logical mind, are by no means exemplified in the same way, although we frequently find them in the same writing. Intuitive judgment or deduction by intuition, is evinced rather by the separation of letters in a word, but the deductive power is evinced by the sequence of letters denoting sequence of ideas—a joining of the letters in a word; and, as in the case already explained under CULTIVATION, an union of words, also indicating JUDGMENT (*q.v.*). Deduction (power of deduction) is then indicated by the *liaison* of words and letters. We need not give another example—that on page 45, already referred to, is sufficient.

VI.—Of Eccentricity, Economy, Egotism, Eloquence, Energy, and Extravagance.

We will now pass on to ECCENTRICITY, which may be deemed the equivalent of the more expressive term BIZARRERIE. If the reader has understood our previous chapter he will be prepared for the evidences of Eccentricity, and look for some oddity or originality, or out of the way form of capital letters and general style. This will be found in the writing of all eccentric people; very often these indications will be found in the writings of highly imaginative and clever people. The capital of the annexed Christian name, "Marie," will give us some indication of Originality and Eccentricity with much vivacity and considerable critical power. The owner of the name is quite unknown to me, and I hope she will pardon the illustration.

An English and a French specimen of eccentric forms of letters, are annexed.

ECONOMY we have already treated under Avarice. The signs of this virtue are evident—a carefulness of ink and space. We frequently see handwriting in which Economy seems allied with a wish for display—a spacing out of lines, a desire to shine perhaps. This is one of the cases in which Economy is the result of training. Circumstances and necessity have compelled Economy where the natural bent of the mind is to spend money—not very extravagantly perhaps, but still to make a good display, with a natural generosity of mind, and every desire to be liberal. The economical training is shown, and prudence bids the individual stay his hand. Such a writing is underneath. Here we find liberal spaces, no meanness, no *petty economy*, but a good economy! The letters are clear and distinct, the intelligence is high, the deductive power great, perseverance considerable, and Economy, the economy of principle, decided. There is no waste, nor disorder; though the writing is hasty there is no swagger—the lines are rigidly honest and generous in appearance; but Economy is practised, we believe; prudence and caution are combined with generous feeling. Some temporary indisposition is manifest.

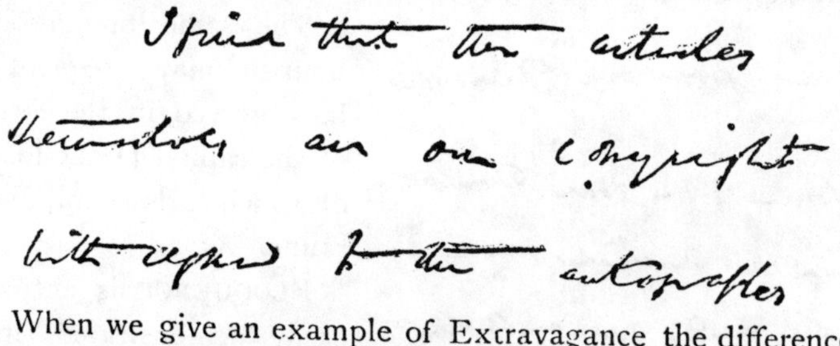

When we give an example of Extravagance the difference will be immediately evident. For this comparison, consult page 57.

EGOTISM has already been touched upon in our reference to the letters *m* and *n*, which when curved backward, indicate a certain amount of Egotism. The much-looped small *d*, is also an indication of self-sufficiency. Whenever the Graphologist perceives the curling *d*, and the flourish, he can safely predicate egotistic ideas in the writer's mind, and if with these tendencies carelessness and *laisser faire* be evident, that man or woman will always believe himself or herself *unappreciated*, and will be disappointed and dissatisfied. As a consequence he (or she) will lose work or employment and become a rolling stone or literary hack with talents sufficient to have performed great things. The "snail-shell" flourish is *pretension*, however humble the manner and unobtrusive the mien.

We have here no specimen amongst our correspondence which we can use to show our meaning; but a foreign example will perhaps suffice. We will only display the curved, clever but egotistic *d*'s, and the flourish which, together, are sufficient indications of egotism. The egotistic *d* must not be confounded with the more simple form of the *d*, which is the sign-manual of Imagination and Ideality.

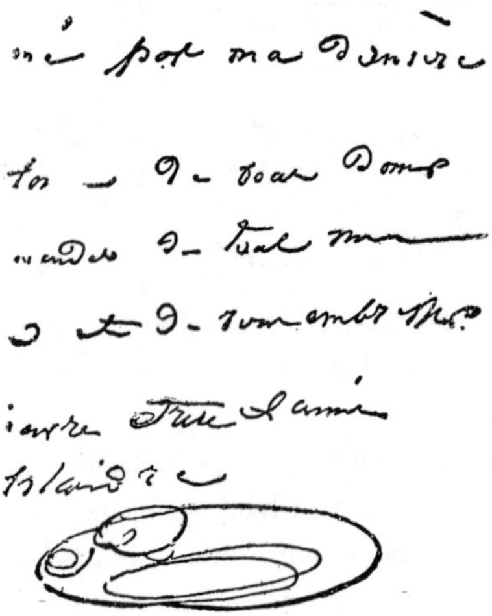

The same pretentious flourish may frequently be observed in the form of the capital D, the loop of which curls round and round.

ELOQUENCE is not so easily demonstrated, for several points have to be considered. We must have talent and cleverness—critical power and judgment with imagination. The intuitive deduction already mentioned is also a factor in the question. So to decide on the handwriting of an eloquent person, as regards his speaking powers, is not always easy. But if the writing disclose critical faculty, imagination, and logical sequence of ideas in the unity of words and letters, we may fairly say that the person has the gift of speaking. Talent will be seen in the curving small *d*, which is united with the subsequent letter in many instances; and no notice need be taken of the *direction* of the handwriting, whether sloping or upright. The points to consider are—intelligence, logic, and criticism, clearness of handwriting, the joining of letters, and also their separation in some words. To illustrate this, we give the writing of MIRABEAU, which shows

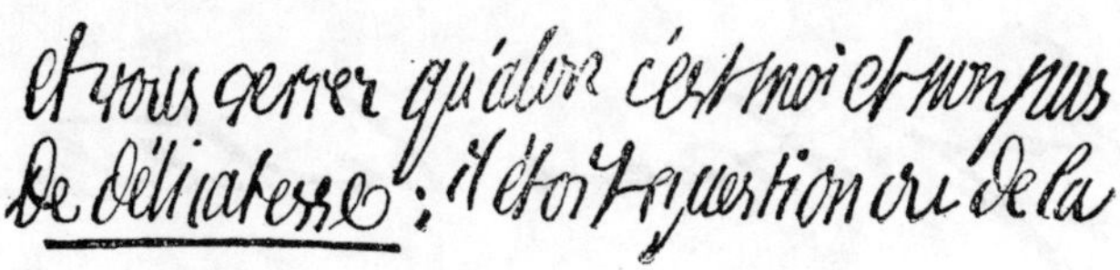

connected ideas; and of JULES FAVRE, which shows *critical* oratory; the former having words joined, the latter having

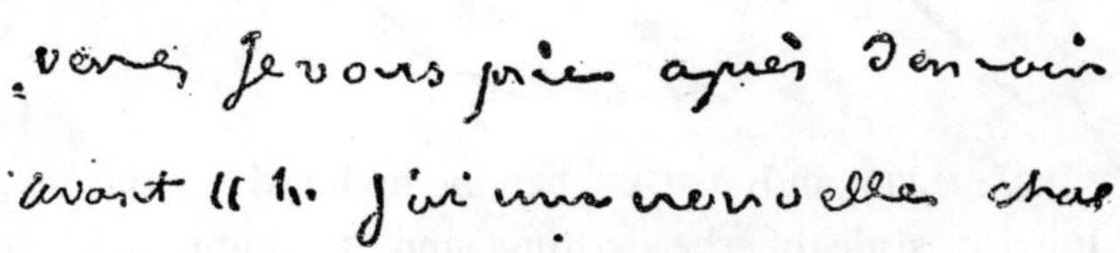

words and letters separated. There is a great deal of sensuousness in the writing of Mirabeau.

ENERGY is an attribute which is easy to perceive, and no lengthened description is necessary to make it familiar. Our own sense will tell us an Energetic handwriting. It is allied to Ardour and Ambition. The writing is firm, rather angular, and sometimes ascending; the *t*'s are well crossed, and high up, sometimes over the letters, and of rather lengthened stroke, indicating Perseverance. There is firmness perceptible, no softness or laziness. There may be wanting the high loops and curves of ENTHUSIASM; but the latter is the fringe, whereas the former (ENERGY) is the substance. The enthusiast is more of the sentimentalist, and his writing will partake of such feelings. The energetic man may be energetic in many ways, but he will show determination and firmness even in pursuit of pleasure. Here is Energy.

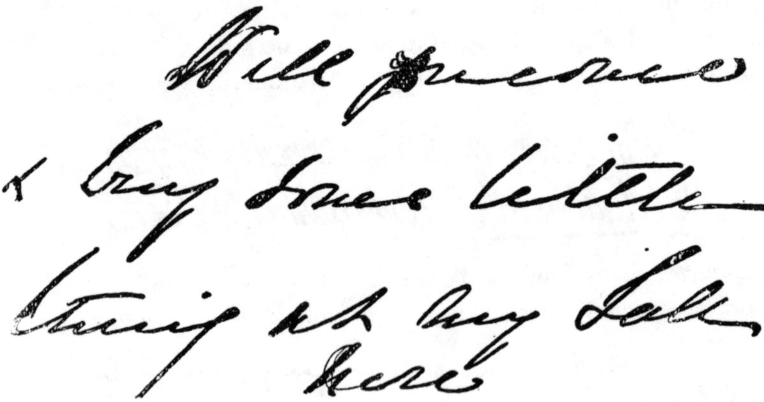

EXCITABILITY and ANGER can be deduced by the generally hurried style of the writing and its angularity. The letters are uneven. There is a want of calmness and finish in the caligraphy. The *t*'s are generally crossed hastily upwards and high; and the writing is frequently thick and very decided; of course, it may also slope, in which case you will expect tenderness and kindness, but also capability for "tempers" when occasion offers. Despotic excitability will have its *t*'s crossed low, and long, firmly; but mere eccentric excitement will be "queer" in its displays—hasty, and with uneven letters in words, while the long decided crosses of the *t*'s will tell us the *temper*. Reason writes clearly and evenly, so, on the contrary, an excitable person will dash off his letter, and even in calmer moments he will betray himself by his mannerisms. The terminals are frequently like sword-points in the irritable, excitable writing, and the *t*'s crossed with an upward and decided bar.

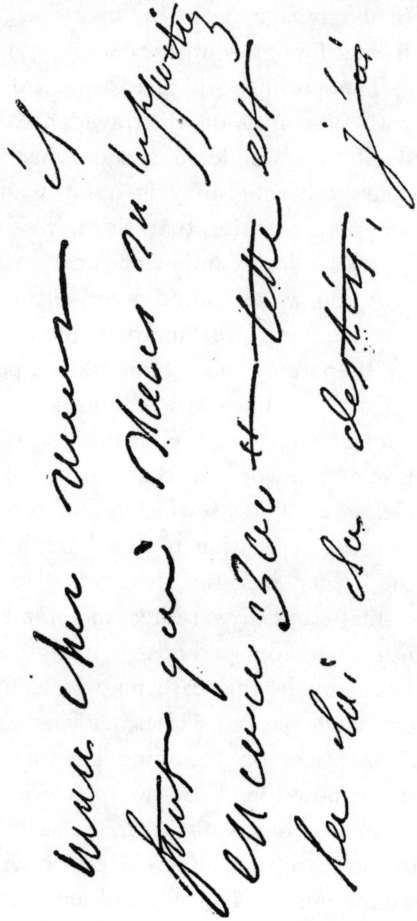

EXTRAVAGANCE and LIBERALITY, or GENEROSITY, are all varied forms of the same impulse, and in a descending scale. The characteristic of an extravagant person will be anticipated. He will be prodigal of pen, ink, and paper—he will take up space; he has grand ideas, so he will sprawl in a somewhat careless way over the paper, write probably a large hand, and omit cautious dots and dashes, though the determined will may be accentuated. Liberality and Generosity, in the spending sense, will be modified specimens of the same forms of handwriting. Generosity being particularly distinguishable by the rounded curves to the finals, and their continued sweep upward. As I have no specimen of Extravagance in my own correspondence, I have cut one from a foreign source. (*See* p. 57.)

The specimen will give the idea of writing which is associated with Liberality and Extravagance. When the indications of "self" are visible in a somewhat generous writing, that is, when the caligraphy is upright and the terminals flowing, we may premise that the individual is generous in cases where his own enjoyment is concerned.

Again, we often find a very economical handwriting spaced out, the lines are far apart, the words are equi-distant, and well separated too. How can we possibly unite these characteristics? They are contradictory, you will say, at first glance. But no; the meaning is plain enough. The separation of the words in that clear equi-distant fashion indicates clearness of ideas which some term Lucidity of Mind (*q.v.*). But the separation of the lines, in my opinion, means that the writer has the desire to "do things well," to make a display, and live rather in grand style, but *circumstances forbid it*, or perhaps a stingy feeling is predominant. Economy in this case may be compulsory; honour forbids extravagance, but wishes, and perhaps past days of ease leave their traces on the mind, and, of course, are reproduced in the handwriting. So we perceive that Extravagance may be in the blood, as it were. The following specimen will illustrate my meaning. Here it will be perceived we have a clear mind, a logical mind, no Extravagance; indeed, there are plain traces and indications of Economy in the finals—yet in the spaces there is Generosity. The person who wrote this must have had an excellent idea of getting the worth of his money. He would not be stingy, but he would have what he paid for and maintain his points.

fledged". I must sincerely say that
I feel very much indebted to you
for all you have done for me and
I ask you to accept my sincere
and warmest thanks!

Perhaps a better specimen is that on page 38, over Bashfulness. The wide spaces there are plain, and while there is no trace of stinginess there is saving. Things well done but no waste.

CHAPTER III.

I.—CONCERNING FALSEHOOD, FINESSE, FLATTERY, ETC

THE next traits upon our list are those arranged under the letter F. Of some we have already treated. FALSEHOOD, for instance, may be regarded in the same light as DECEIT. FIRMNESS is only another term for DETERMINATION. FEROCITY has been touched upon under ANGER. So we will content ourselves with merely detailing the indications, and pass on to the others in this chapter.

FALSEHOOD is shown in writing by indistinctness and wavy lines, threads of ink doing duty for a succession of letters. People who write thus are not to be trusted to keep their words. FINESSE is not Falsehood, though, and should not be confounded with it. (See also UNTRUTHFULNESS.)

FIRMNESS is a decided writing, *t*'s well barred, and a strong stroke at end. The annexed specimen is one of firmness with good nature.

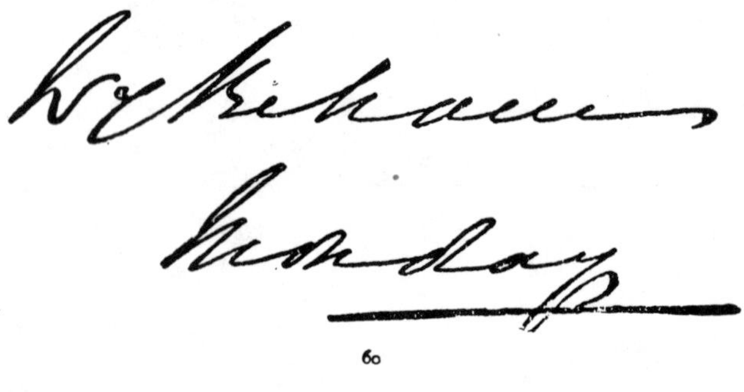

FEROCITY is merely energetic Cruelty, an impulse, and therefore Anger with Impulsiveness and Selfishness will be evident. Thick writing and strongly barred *t*'s with upright style.

FACILITY of composition, or of writing, is easily recognised in the equally sustained words and lines running on and frequently joined. Such a hand is shown under "Extravagance with Economy," on page 59. The ideas flow quickly, and the pen glides rapidly over the paper.

FATALITY is shown by a persistent downward slope of the writing. In many cases the slope is corrected, and the writing mounts a while, but again it falls, and we feel that the germ of the fatal illness is already putting forth shoots, and will undermine the constitution. For obvious reasons no specimen of this writing is annexed.

FINESSE is visible in the majority of handwritings: it is sometimes very strongly accentuated, sometimes faintly, as "tact," sometimes the writing is extremely "diplomatic."

This is a perfectly legitimate attribute, for true Finesse will not degenerate into lying or hypocrisy. Words are smaller at the end than at the beginning, the letters dwindle away. Here is the *tendency* to throw dust in people's eyes, but such people do not deceive you, though we must confess that Finesse is not strict frankness in dealing. It is taking advantage of circumstances and knowledge of affairs, what is termed "business capacity." Some writers develop Finesse even to the verge of deceit; and the *undulating* uneven letters will give the clue.

FLATTERY is noticeable in a somewhat similar manner. Finesse comes in here again, but the writing will be of a meaner and less noble character—a hand which indicates a kind of meanness, a petty trivial hand with the signs of extreme tact. There is want of dignity in the writing, and possibly a want of truth. But a considerable amount of practical knowledge is necessary to arrive at this conclusion, for, at the best, it is a complicated characteristic.

After having mentioned the signs of Finesse, Diplomacy and Deceit, Frankness will be very easily perceived. Clearness and honesty of purpose in distinct and even writing, well-formed letters, and open words, will prepare us for Frankness. Courage, Firmness, and Decision are present. The letters will be of the same elevation in the words, which do not terminate in sharp points, but rather in rounded curves. Clear, plain, equal letters of sustained size are the principal signs of Frankness—a common sense delineation.

II.—Of Generosity, Gentleness, and Grandeur, Etc.

Generosity again is allied with other attributes. We have already touched upon this virtue ; but, as we remarked previously, there is a generosity of the mind as well as generosity of the hand. The man may be generous as regards his money, and ill-tempered, and may possess other unpleasant attributes, but the generously-minded man is frank and loyal, his writing will be open, rounded, and have curling finals : the *m*'s and *n*'s will be written like *u*'s, in good-natured fashion ; clearness and open-handed writing are the characteristics of your generous friend ; of course, the truly generous man has self-control. So you will not find his penmanship sprawling and careless. He will be benevolent, but not without caution. A truly generous man was the "Great Earl of Shaftesbury ;" he was generous in the truest sense, but he did not give alms indiscriminately. His tender, sloping handwriting was

The Baroness Burdett-
Coutts presents her
compliments and begs
to thank Messrs. Ward
Lock &c for their
politeness in forwarding
her the pretty book
of Chats about Animals.
The Baroness would be
glad to know at what
price they propose selling
their book - as she would
like to recommend it
Stratton St.
November 1878

tempered with caution and critical power, while the crossing of the *t*'s high, hinted at some quickness of temper and irritation.

GENTLENESS is a characteristic trait which demands some little study. We have the well-rounded curves of Benevolence, the parallel lines and clearness of Simplicity, and the "turning tails" to *y*'s and *g*'s. The writing will also slope, and there will not be many *t*'s barred strongly. There is no real want of will, however; there is firmness enough, but a rounded softness of character which will ally itself with unselfishness.

The handwriting given on page 63 displays great tenderness and good-nature, with considerable firmness and some reserve. But the flowing *l*'s and looped letters, generally indicate a generous, kindly, nature with no extravagance; and a straight-forwardness and directness which are admirable.

GRANDEUR and Ostentation are visible in the general masterly large letters, with wide spaces between lines and a kind of careless magnificence not easy to describe. There is always a certain amount of pretension in such writing, if the mind is vulgar, but the person "born to the purple" will write a simple, unaffected, large, bold hand, with wide spaces and no curling *d*'s, or flourishes. So Ostentation can be seen in vulgar flourish. True Grandeur in the bold simple style of assured position. There is a good deal of this grandeur with pretension in the accompanying writing of Louis Philippe. The reader will note the curling flourish which speaks of "egotism" to the Graphologist, but there is something regal in its lines, even though there is some trace of vulgarity.

This signature is a *fac simile* of that appended to his abdication, and shows the determination to pose as a monarch to the last.

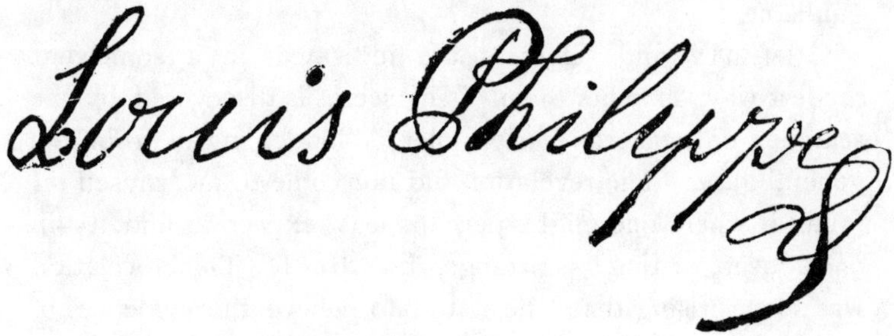

III.—Of Honesty, Humility, Hypocrisy, and Heroism.

We can now pass on to Honesty and such other qualities which are included under the initial H. Honesty and Honour, as honourable feelings may, for all practical purposes, be classed together. If he will turn back to Candour, the reader will see how that virtue is illustrated. That Honesty and Candour are allied to each other any one will admit, and the same specimen of caligraphy will suit us for illustration; the same evenness of letters, the straight lines as in the letter already given on page 41. Indeed, as we remarked when dealing with that letter, the straightforwardness of the writer is admirable. There is directness in every line, no subterfuge or *finesse* even. A strict code of honour is evidenced, plain dealing in all events.

Thus Honour is shown by the equal spaces between words and lines, and the general even handwriting. Of course, many other attributes will be perceived in honourable hands, even distasteful characteristics may be recognised, temper, stinginess and what not; but at present we are only concerned with the indications of honourable conduct; and in the writing under the headings of CANDOUR and GENEROSITY the reader will find the necessary sign-types for his guidance.

HUMILITY and Shyness are indicated in a somewhat modest way, as befits them. The secret is discovered by the searcher only, as the early violet is hidden away from the general gaze. The revelation did not come to me, myself: I found it where one might perhaps least expect to find it—in one's own writing! Strange, but true! This revelation was so surprising that I hesitated to believe the evidences of my senses at first, but further experience has confirmed the impression, and I will tell you the secret. It lies in a nutshell, or rather in the capital letter M, and in the proportion of the letters to each other. Of course there are degrees of HUMILITY. There is the true self-respecting virtue and the slavish bowing down. But the first view of one's Modesty is in the M.

When we find our M's of pretty equal form, I mean when the strokes forming the letter, whether two strokes or three, are of equal height and rather close together, we may safely pronounce the writer modest and rather shy in society. This may appear in some natures contradictory, but my attention was first drawn to the investigation of the M by an experience.

I was delineating a certain writing, and hazarded the conjecture, for I was not certain, that the writer was of a rather timid nature and wanting in self-confidence. A laugh resulted. My pronouncement was ridiculed because it appeared that the gentleman whose handwriting had been submitted was particularly "cheeky," and had a measure of "impudence," astonishing in one so young. But some perceptive person remarked, to my intense relief—"I think half his assurance is assumed; he used to be very shy—and I believe" added the lady, "that the lad's impudence is really the result of self-consciousness, and a desire not to appear shy!"

This turned out to be the case. The writing was rather pressed in and the various letters preserved a kind of relative size, which, I believe, is typical of a modest temperament. There is some further experience to be gained in this point, but, so far, the usual indications have proved correct in a general way, and show an absence of what is termed, popularly, "nasty pride." Self-respect is displayed, also in something of the same manner. But of this anon. An unobtrusive writing is timid and retiring. Simplicity and absence of ostentation and flourish are noticeable.

HYPOCRISY is a terrible thing to deal with in a book on Graphology, because it is not pleasant to give illustrations of it, and we are unable to do so, for we have no such writing in our possession. The only way in which we can show the contrast between the honest and the dishonest, is to compare two specimens of foreign origin. In the former we perceive frankness and clearness, in the latter dissimulation and hypocrisy. The ways of the hypocrite are varied and tortuous, and when he is off his guard, his writing will also be wavy and tortuous. In this lies the solution, but if he be a thorough dissembler he cannot easily be found out save in the signature. Here he may be detected, for unless he be very dodgy indeed, a man seldom varies his signature, never unless he has some very particular reason for it—some idea that his writing may come up in evidence against him some day! Such men write continually differing hands, and change their writing from deliberate design and intention. This is hypocrisy in its most dangerous form. Whoever "forged" the signature to a now famous letter of "15th May," did the

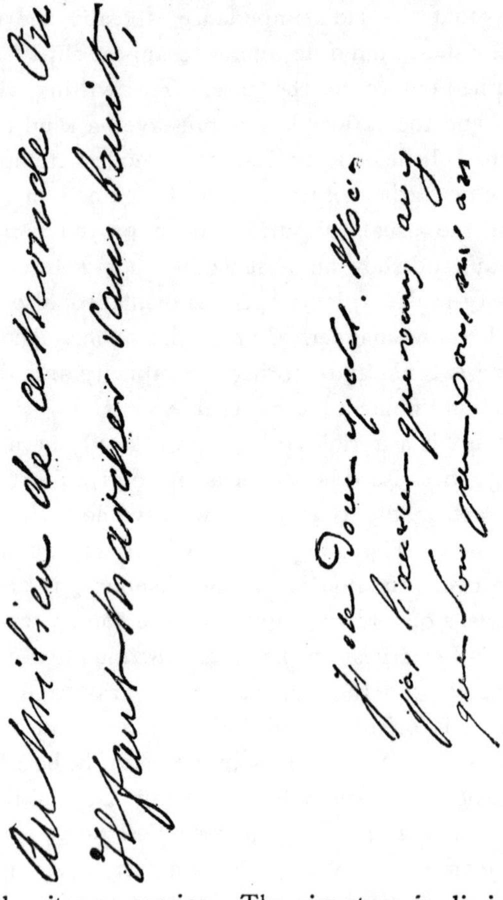

suggested writer no service. The signature is dissimulative, tortuous, dodgy, and diplomatic in the extreme, as any student of Graphology can see at a glance. Concerning the authorship we offer no opinion ; having our own we mean to keep it. The two specimens of handwriting referred to above are annexed. There can be little doubt as regards the better character. The first is an open, frank, penmanship ; but the second is tortuous and dissimulative—untrustful.

In HEROISM we have unselfishness and kindliness with ardour and firmness. This characteristic, therefore, must be sought for " between the lines " of the writing.

There are various attributes to be looked for in this connection, for a man may be very quiet and reserved, or very courageous and warlike, or demonstrative. But the qualities generally linked with Heroism are firmness, coolness, endurance, self-sacrifice, unselfishness. So we shall have a rather sloping, firm hand ; *t*'s crossed, in a somewhat ardent writing, with, probably, the *a*'s and *o*'s closed up, as a sign of self-control; and the rounded curves of Generosity, and often the loops and signs of Imagination.

Why ? you may inquire. Because, in the first place, you will require sympathy to become heroic—you must have a fellow-feeling for your friend. To do this you must put yourself in his place, and must therefore not lack imagination. You must be forgetful of self—not egotistical—so the writing must slope. The ascendant lines indicate Ardour, Courage, Enthusiasm—and thus by deduction we reach self-abnegation, which is devotion—true loyalty—Heroism.

We can now continue our list under the next letter. Ill-health need not again be commented on. It is often allied with Despondency and Melancholy, and is seen in sloping, careless, weak writing, with the unfortunate descending movement. The ill-health may be counteracted by will, and the mind may, and frequently does, assert itself over the hand.

The commencement is perhaps sloping upwards, or straight, but the langour of body wins at last, and the writing falls.

Such an instance is annexed. Here we have the energetic actress Rachel, her strong will, her imagination, sensitiveness, and ambition with economy. But we have also ill-health and melancholy in the descending writing. She was about to seek health in the warmth of Egypt, where she traced the lines we have appended. There again is "fatality," a symptom shown clearly in the signature of Prince Rudolph of Austria some time before his death.

IV.—Of Indecision, Imagination, Indolence, Jealousy, Etc.

Indecision is shown in the varying sizes of letters and words, and, as may be expected, a want of such signs as point to firmness of purpose. In diplomatic writing we perceive firmness with undulating letters, in Indecision we have undulating writing without firmness. There is no necessity to give an illustration.

Imagination and Impulsiveness may be placed together, for the same character of handwriting will give both traits. Impulse is a sudden effort of mind, and Imagination is also indicated by certain flying letters, the capitals being particularly noticeable. But in addition the Imaginative writer is frequently indistinct, yet his letters are long, the capitals are large and elegant in cultivated minds. The true test of the imaginative faculty being the small *d*, curved and generally joined to the next letter in the same word. As already explained in our opening chapter, the imaginative person hurries over his work, his hand tries to catch his ideas, and illegibility is the result. If to this partial illegibility we find a poetic or artistic taste in graceful and original capitals, we may rest assured that we have a hurried writer, a man who is fired by his brain and wishes to strike while the iron is hot.

But there are also people of great powers of imagination who write plainly and more calmly. These are they of colder and more calculating temperament, people of more orderliness and circumspection, and of less liberality and generosity; people very fond of *minutiæ* and detail—polishers of phrases, and of MS.; people who do excellent work, really more solid work that your flyaway romancer. The quick writer, the man or woman of much novel-writing, is generally indistinct. The brain works quickly, and the hand must follow. This is the case with many living and dead writers, whose autographs we have seen. Not one writes, or wrote, a distinct hand. Can the penmanship of Charles Reade, Miss Braddon, "Ouida," James Payn, Walter Thornbury, Dickens, Kingsley, Wilkie Collins, Daudet, Madox Brown, Anthony Trollope, and many others we could name, be characterized as clear and "good" writing, so far as legibility is concerned? It may look neat and even; but the letters appear very unformed to the unassisted vision. We are referring to those authors who write continually. But those who do not hurry into print so much, such as the late George Eliot, and others who are content with a more deliberate production, we find more legible.

Artists, painters, actors, and authors of vivid imagination, generally write in this manner; and we annex a few specimens, to illustrate our meaning. The method and order of the one class are lost in the hurry and impulsiveness of the other. A clear hand is no evidence of want of imagination; it merely argues a more methodical and calmer imagination, a better regulated brain.

Some of the signatures annexed are written better than the body of the letters to which they respectively appertain; and in publishing them, we only add a tribute to the imagination of the authors, and in no way detract from their many excellent qualities.

Note the movement and "go" in this signature of Victor Hugo, the turn of the small *d*'s, and the critical power of the separated letters, giving also observation.

Here again is De Balzac. See the great imagination in the *d* and the originality in the B.

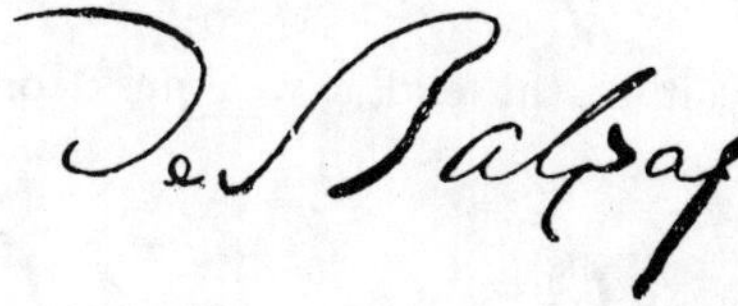

Next we have the autographs of the Dumas, *père et fils*. The father first, as is natural.

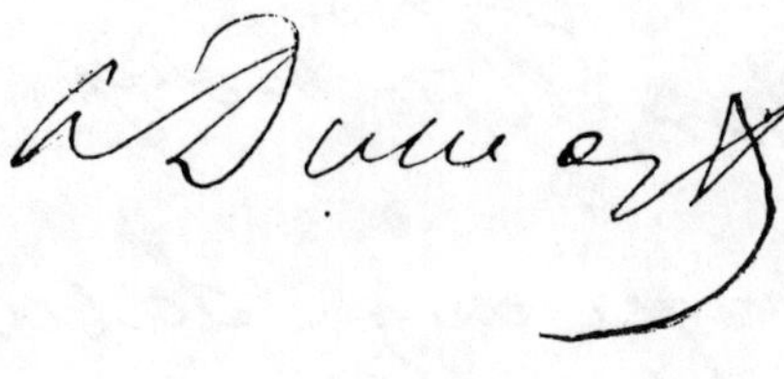

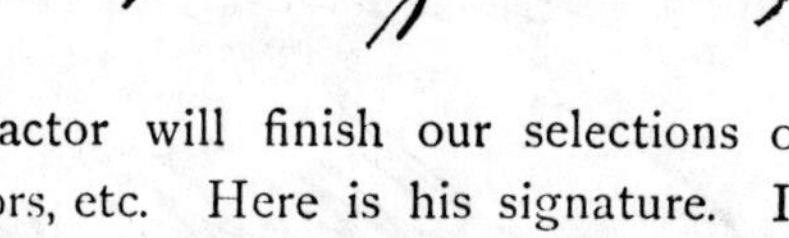

Talma the celebrated actor will finish our selections of French imaginative authors, etc. Here is his signature. It is not very easy to decipher it, nor the writing which precedes it. But imagination is accentuated in the T, and in the little

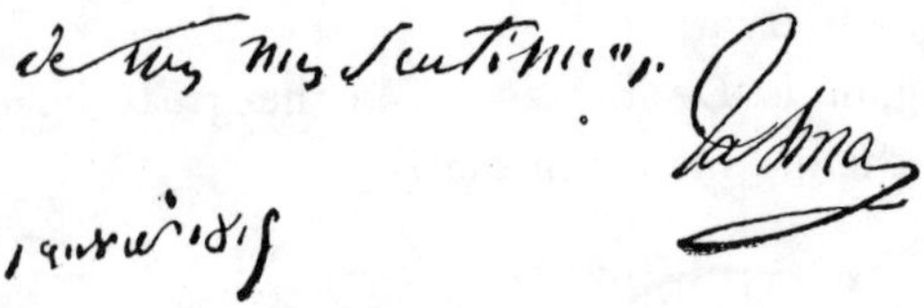

flourish of conceit at the end, a weakness common to most actors and actresses.

We now pass on to some English autographs with the view of sustaining our remarks about illegibility and talent. Here is the signature of the late Walter Thornbury, from whom I received several letters in times past, all of which necessitated considerable study to decipher, as the reader will judge from the signature.

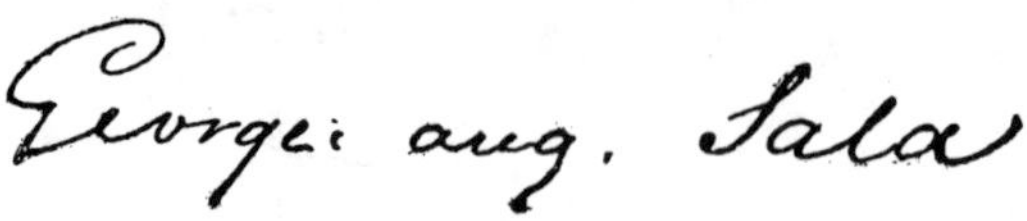

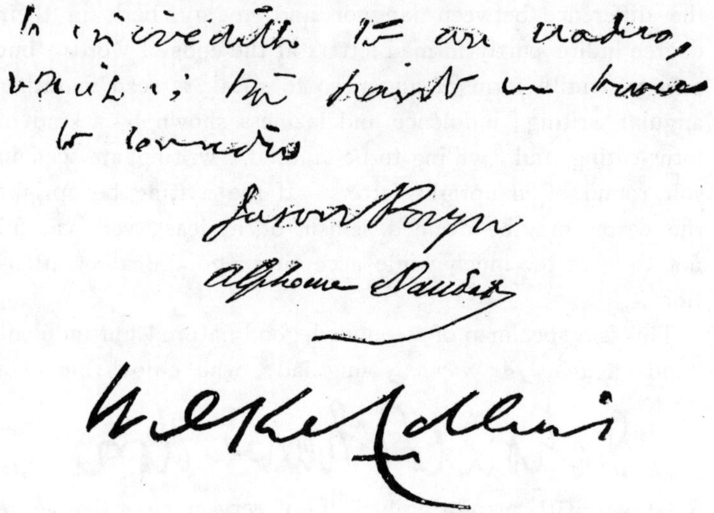

Compare the caligraphy of the rapid and essentially imaginative writer with the clear steady handwriting of Mr. Sala whose methodical manner of composing is well known, and see whether Graphology has not some basis of truth and reason for those who will read. Look at the care and caution displayed by G. A. Sala, and the hurried, almost illegible, scrawl of poor harassed Walter Thornbury!

We think we have now demonstrated the difference between the imaginative rapid writer and the painstaking and more methodical author.

INDOLENCE is characterized by a softness and sensuousness of writing. We know energy is expressed by rapidity of style and some firmness; but your indolent person, your lotus eater, is of sensuous temperament, and lazy, so you will have rounded turns to the letters, and even in many cases these rounded terminals will not be fully fledged. Here lies the difference between languor and energy, both in their degree indite partly-formed letters at the ends of words ; but energy, a mild form of anger, so to speak, is seen in rather angular writing ; indolence and laziness shown by a kind of lotus-eating, and "willing-to-be-amused," writing are seen in soft, round, often upright, letters. If the writing be upright the writer may be deemed selfish, or, at least, very careful not to give too much while accepting a good deal of attention.

This is a specimen of a rounded, good-natured, but indolent hand—a *dolce far niente* young lady, who enjoys life in a

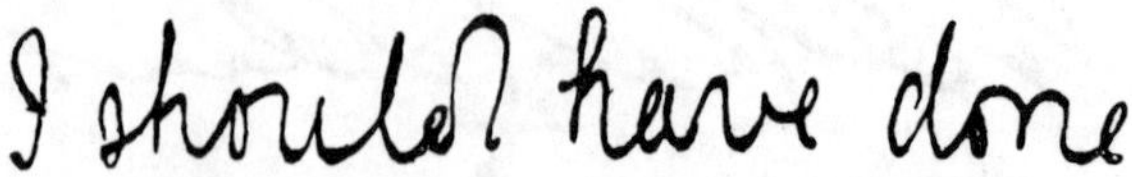
I should have done

quiet way without putting herself out very much, a temperate mind, with great unconscious capability of arousing affection, but not herself much disturbed, as a rule.

The INTELLIGENT hand is marked by a general harmony and frequently elegance in the writing. There is a coolness and determination in the penmanship, a clearness and some imagination. The bold bright intellect is evident in the hand-

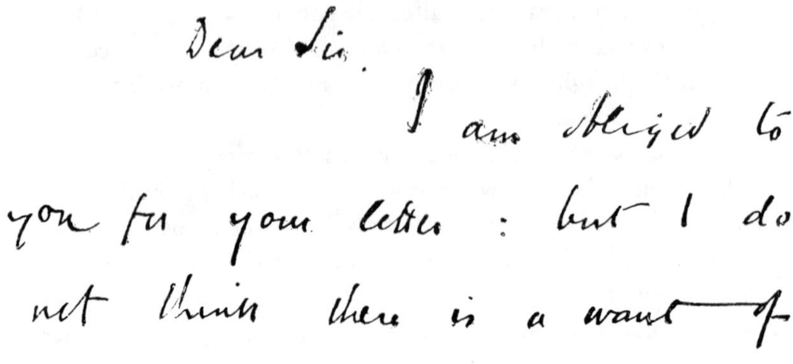
Dear Sir,
I am obliged to you for your letter : but I do not think there is a want of

writing of Fénélon. The lucidity of mind in his caligraphy is remarkable. But there are other and more subtle intellects —the intellect of the business man, with some originality and great lucidity of mind. The writer is unknown to me, personally, and I hope he will excuse the extract being shown. (See p. 76.)

Underneath is the poetic intelligence, with energy.

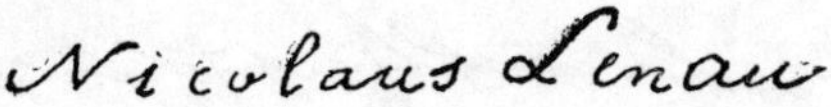

Here is intelligence of the highest order; frankness, clear-

ness, simplicity, all marked. The same characteristics will

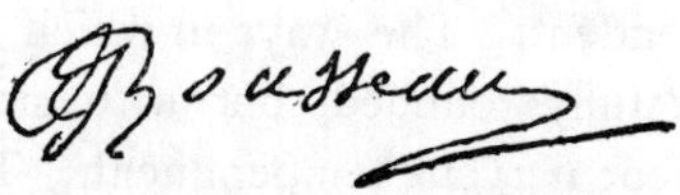

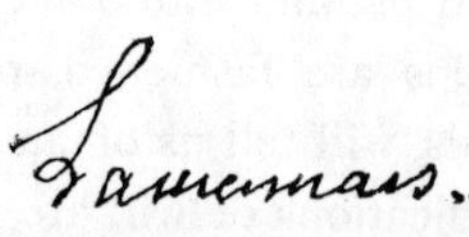

be observed in the writing of other talented authors; see the signatures of Rousseau, Lamennais and our own poet Browning.

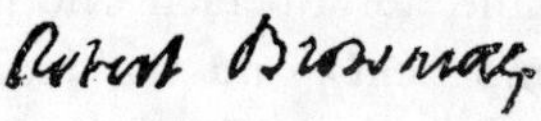

There is also a less pleasing side to the picture—a second-rate intelligence, as we can perceive from the signature of Lenau, when he was out of his mind in some degree; and from another autograph, which we will not give, we could show the want of ideas in the vulgar, feeble will, and narrow-minded capitals.

There are, of course, degrees in intelligence, as in every

other attribute. We have given the general characteristics, and the modifications will be found by our readers. We give a foreign specimen of weak will and want of intellectuality.

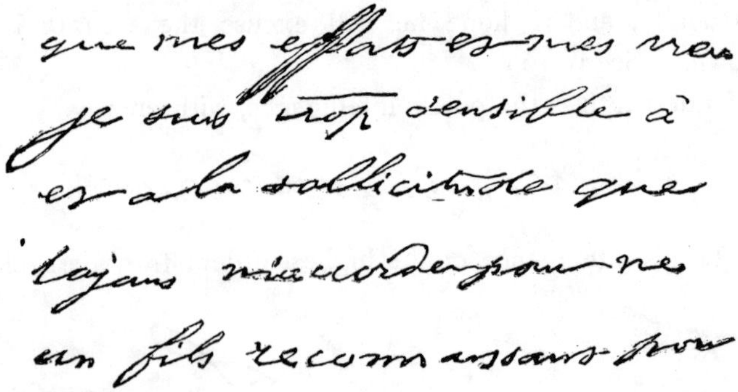

IMPATIENCE will be found associated with impulse and haste. The crossing of the *t* when above the letter, or when hurriedly made, will naturally lead us to ascribe impatience and petulance to our correspondent. The ways in which the stops are fashioned, not carefully rounded, but with small tails, will tell us of an impatient nervous temperament. The indications of will are not very strong in the really impatient hand (for a person who possesses self-control is not outwardly impatient), and the indications of firmness and decision are consequently faint.

We may now pass on to a somewhat complicated attribute. It is nevertheless a very common trait in character; but it requires dissection. We mean JEALOUSY.

In Physiognomy, Jealousy is found in the brows; in Graphology it is perceived in the weakness and sentimentality of the writing. Every one tells us that we cannot find jealousy unless we first have the love; that jealousy is an excess of love. Well, then, all excess is weakness. That is a fact in Graphology as in other things. Thus we may fairly look for extra tenderness and sentiment in a handwriting of one who is likely to be jealous, and particularly causelessly jealous. So we must first ascertain whether tenderness and affection predominate in the handwriting.

If so, we shall have a very sloping hand, and long-looped *l*'s, *y*'s, and *g*'s. This is love and romantic regard. The person is also impulsive, and rather given to leap to conclusions. Now jealousy is begotten of a kind of self-consciousness and want of faith. No self-contained, self-assured person will give way to jealousy. The person must possess a great imagination, and build castles on a very slight foundation. We must look there for traces of egotism, imagination, tenderness and sentiment, and impulse. We must look for sloping writing and looped letters, a fly-away bar to the *t*, but not necessarily a *weak* bar, because jealous persons are obstinate to a certain extent. We shall not find any very great signs of intellectuality, not the large frank writing of Féñélon, for example, in the hands of jealous people.

Jealousy is a weakness to a certain point, and, as we have endeavoured to show, rather a complicated weakness. It has its phases, like other passions, and in the light-hearted will have a short life; but in the melancholy, taciturn, self-examining, temperament, if the writing be rather thick, or descending, or cruel, then jealousy will work as it did in Othello, and "trifles light as air" will be "confirmation strong as Holy Writ." "Beware, my lord, of jealousy!"

JUDGMENT is another complicated attribute in Graphology, and will require some little detailed explanation. There are, as already mentioned, two kinds of Judgment—the intuitive and the deductive, and these two are frequently found united in the same handwriting. Observation must be present with the intuitive critical power; and the joining of the letters of a word (often the joining of words together) gives us what is termed the "logical sequence of ideas," a power of tracing and following out; reasoning power, in fact. The power of seizing upon the salient points of a case and criticising them is good; but the deduction must be right to be of any use; so when we find the separated letters in some words, and the sequence of ideas in the connected letters existing in the same handwriting, we may fairly assume that the writer possesses an excellent judgment, and reasoning power, which will control imagination, and give his opinion weight; in fact, he will weigh both sides of an argument, and give you an unbiassed opinion.

The annexed specimen is a very good type of the judgment which should be possessed by publishers. The writing shows excellent qualities, criticism, and deductive powers, with considerable cultivation and talent. I trust the writer will pardon my candour, and the use of his writing.

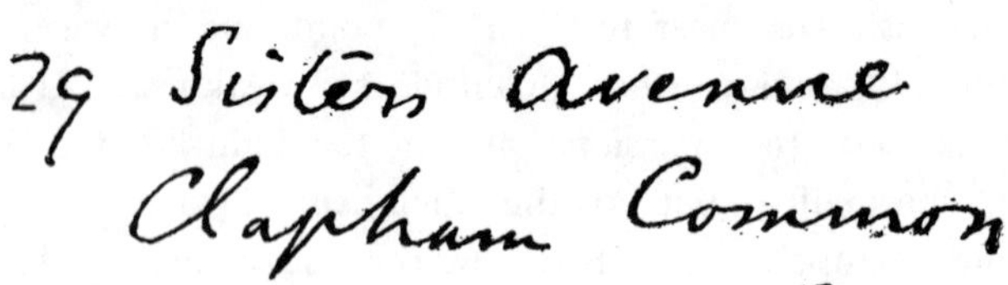

This shows excellent judgment.

JOCOSITY is a very pleasing trait in any handwriting, and can be deduced from the imagination with turned up finals which indicate wit. You will often find considerable eccentricity in the forms of the letters in the jocose, dry, witty man. The spirit of fun is very decided in the accompanying writing, but allied with considerable will and obstinacy with generous instincts, and quick temper.

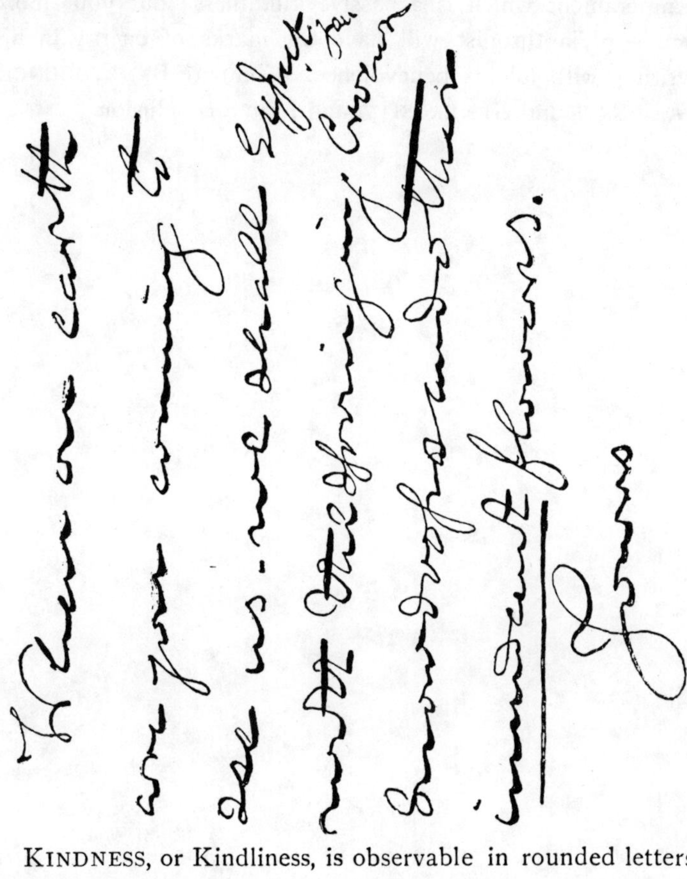

KINDNESS, or Kindliness, is observable in rounded letters We may find it associated with very tender writing, that is sloping writing, and also in the more upright hand. Goodness and generosity will be found allied with kindness of heart. The letters generally are of almost equal height, and their roundedness tell us of the kindly good-tempered hand and being. The kindness may arise from an easy-going temperament which is a passive kindliness; but your more active philanthropist will have the marks of energy in his writing, with all his benevolence. Compare BENEVOLENCE, GOODNESS and GENEROSITY, and form a conclusion.

CHAPTER IV.

I.—OF LAZINESS, LOGIC, LUCIDITY, LOVE, AND LOYALTY.

WE must pass on in this Chapter to some other characteristics, keeping in mind our general alphabetical arrangement. The first we shall consider in this part is Laziness.

LAZINESS is a compound of indolence, idleness and indecision, and so we must turn to these failings to arrive at our conclusion. Laziness is a want of energy, so we must not expect to find any of the signs of energy in a lazy person. Energy is distinguished by a firm, often an ascendant style. A rapidity of action in the quick forcible bars to the small *t*'s. There is angularity and movement in the energetic writing.

Now in the lazy hand there is none of this energy. There is a sensuousness in it, a carelessness, a difference in the sizes of letters and a softness in the rounded, rather large and somewhat upright writing. There are no signs of hurry, but languid short terminals with no signs of active imagination or will.

LOGIC is shown by the connected letters and words. We have, when treating of the logical sequence of ideas, already demonstrated the logical mind. The reason and the intelligence are developed, and when the writing is clear and yet with words and letters connected, we find Lucidity of mind as well as Logic. Good speakers generally write hands in which the logical faculty of deduction and criticism are

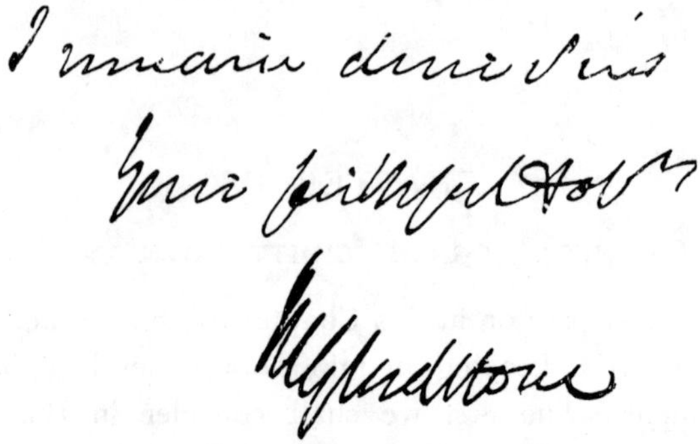

united with some imagination. In statesmen we frequently find these types united with *finesse* and subtlety; and the irregular forms of letters, a serpentine wavy mood, which is eminently characteristic of the tortuous mind.

LUCIDITY OF MIND, *i.e.*, clearness of ideas, is shown in the clear straightforward handwriting—a frank undisguised hand, with the letters sometimes united, but also, although less frequently, separated as by the critical faculty.

LOVE is affection, and as we have already dealt with the latter trait it is hardly necessary for us to indicate the symptoms of Love, or rather the power of loving, in mankind. The sloping writing is tenderness, but if we have the long loops and tenderness with egotism, we wonder at the contrast. Yet the union is not uncommon; it indicates the loving nature which, nevertheless, is exigent, and wants all arrangements made for her *first*.

Love is strong or weak, sentimental, romantic, strong or sensual. The cold-hearted, those who often cause love or admiration in others, and who rather lean towards the opposite sex, have generally upright hands, more or less energetic, with somewhat indolent and economical terminations to words. The thick, rounded, semi-selfishness of this writing, with the will more or less developed, is not a *constant* hand. The love will be strong, even yielding, but temporary, passionate, but not reciprocal for long. You may see the *finesse* in the letters, and the love of ease in the softness and thickness of the writing. There is a short decided way of crossing the *t*'s which is particularly dangerous! If the writing be not so easy going, not so thick, we shall have an affection which, if aroused, will brave all things to gain its ends, a dangerous, because passionate, love hidden beneath a calm, a self-contained exterior, the hidden fire beneath the cold lava, but which will some day break out and overwhelm us.

For other indications of love, see AFFECTION, TENDERNESS, SENSITIVENESS.

LOYALTY may be mentioned here for it possesses indications of tenderness and generosity. With these characteristics we have truthfulness and unselfishness in sloping writing. Such people are true and loyal in love and friendship, as subjects or dependents. Energetic loyalty will be indicated by ardour and a slightly ascending writing with all its roundness and gentleness and *firmness.* For *Lucidity of Ideas*, see under Logic.

II.—OF MAGNIFICENCE, MATHEMATICS, MELANCHOLY, MODESTY, ETC.

MAGNIFICENCE, or Grandeur, is indicated by the size of the writing. People who like grandeur or, at any rate, who would have everything grand about them if they could, generally write large wide hands. The letters have a "magistral" look, and the lines are well apart. If the writer has a very excellent opinion of himself, he will betray his tendencies by the spaces between the down strokes of the letters M, H, etc. The width he leaves between these lines will enable us to gauge the extent of his self-appreciation. There are, naturally, modifications of these indications. There may be meanness allied with display, and the taste for grandeur may be, in practice, modified by avarice or necessary economy. An impecunious peer may have all the natural tastes of his progenitors who may, nevertheless, have left him badly off, and enforced economy may be, therefore, visible in the writing; but, as a rule, it is the actual characteristic, the soul, which is displayed, unless habit has become second nature. Thus we often see how handwriting alters, as cares and responsibilities change the once free, generous, large hand into the more constrained, and apparently, more economical and closer "fist."

A *Mathematical* and scientific person will write a careful hand, the lines will be straight in line, rather small penmanship, with critical tendencies—the tendency of the searcher and the analyst. You will not find any sentimental long "tails" of letters in your scientific man, but you will perceive deductive judgment in the sequence of the letters, as in the annexed signature of Cuvier. Here is the angular writing of penetration, simplicity, connected ideas; but unfortunately a flourish of some pretension connects the terminal of the name, with some rather commonplace taste. But there is ambition in the flourish, which we presume was satisfied when the naturalist was made a baron and his pretensions recognised. There is considerable movement in the signature, more than is often seen in a strictly scientific writer; but then Cuvier did not deal in "dry" figures; he studied natural science, and possessed imagination.

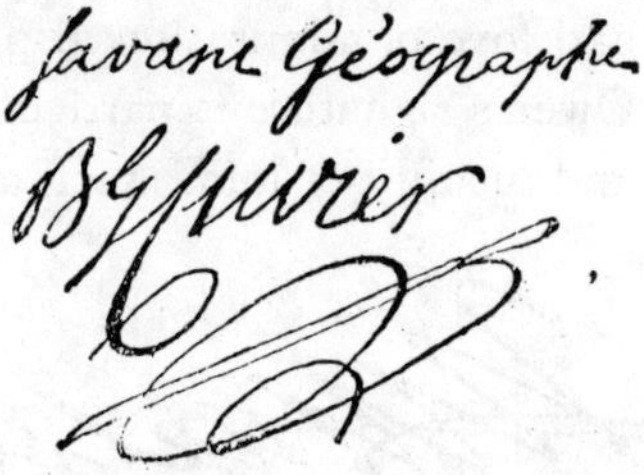

That mathematical and scientific geniuses write in the particular manner claimed for them by Graphology is evident from the dictum of a writer who denies in a great measure the possibility of deducing character from handwriting. The writer says, "The accuracy and precision of the scholar . . . do constantly betray themselves in a type of handwriting so distinct and recognisable as to have earned the title of scholarly."

It must not be supposed, however, that *all* true mathematicians write clear hands, and that no scientific man shows tenderness in his writing. Many mathematicians are very careless, indeed, so perfectly absorbed and wrapped up in calculations, that they "slur" over their writing in a very absent manner. These are the untidy ones who are careless of appearances, their imagination carries them away, and a rapid writing, a more or less indistinguishable hand, is the result. But with scientific men we find the angular *penetrative* character. Witness the signatures below, of Professor Huxley and Owen. We have an autograph by us of Sir James Paget, which shows much tenderness and imagination, with both critical and deductive faculties, considerable originality, neatness and order. There is vivacity and energy in Professor Huxley's autograph, with deductive, logical and critical acumen, great firmness and clearness of mind, and some eccentricity in the capital letter. Here, again, is the movement and "go" observable in the writing of those who study natural sciences. But there is no flourish and love of admiration displayed in the signature. Professor Owen's signature is particularly indicative of connected ideas and lucidity of mind, tact, and imagination.

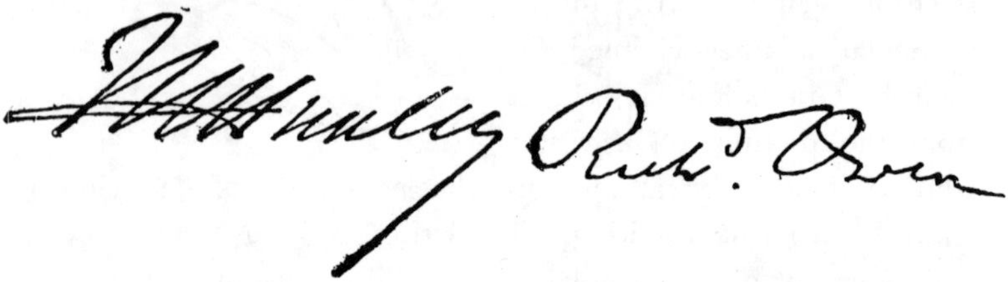

MELANCHOLY—that is, the tendency to melancholy and what some call Fatalism—is exemplified in the continued downward direction of the writing. Ill-health, as already explained, will often account for the falling direction of the writing, but some people possessed of great energy will combat this tendency successfully. Many French and even German writers on Graphology, declare that a downward tendency of the writing indicates a violent death. There can be no doubt that disappointments and ill-success (even in cases of persons who have attained to the summit of their ambition and fallen), are apparent in the descending tendency of writing. This is particularly observable in the cases of both the Emperors Napoleon the First and Third, in the name. The same is observable in the writing of Marie Antoinette, whose signature, shortly before her execution, is appended.

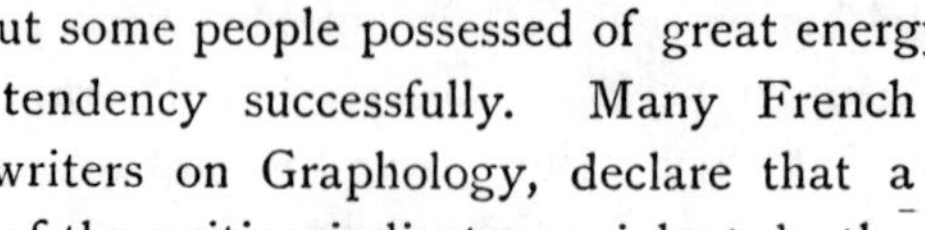

As to the theory of German writers that a continuous downward tendency argues a violent death, a tragic end to life, we can only say that it has lately received confirmation by the death of the late unhappy Rudolf of Austria. Here is his autograph, written some time before any one suspected that his life would be so suddenly cut short in such a terribly tragic way. I have had permission to use this signature, and any student of this work will at once perceive the main characteristics of the unfortunate Prince. The rather thick, sensual writing, is very significant, but *finesse* and imagination with the artistic taste in the capital R are equally positive. What strikes one most is the falling signature and the forecast of trouble which it indicates.

The accompanying autograph of Marie Antoinette is not her last signature. This was written some time before her spirit was thoroughly broken. In this we see the energetic will, striving against misfortune and yet unable finally to conquer it. This shows the struggle with Fate. The other autograph of the ill-fated Queen is of later date and much more sloping. Unfortunately, I have not got a copy of it, but the fact remains. There is in it not even a sign of struggle. She is quite worn out and dispirited, the whole signature falls as greatly as the *ette* in the final word of the signature annexed.

The French theory of "Fate" is again singularly brought out in the case of a person of melancholy temperament who was of a very dreamy mood, and who finished his career by committing suicide. This is a *bonâ fide* instance; the will is curiously accentuated in some words, but the tendency to a violent and tragic end is equally decided in the falling letters.

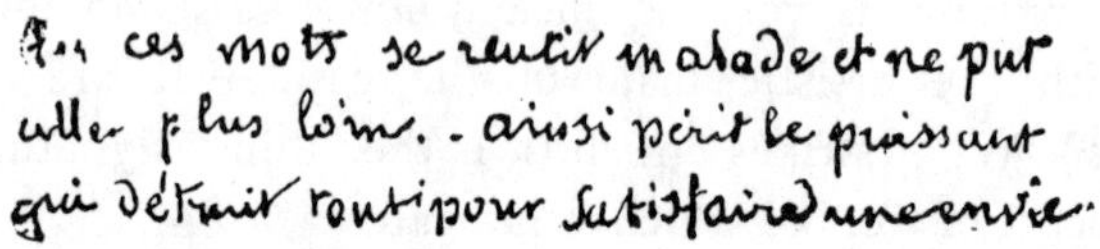
A ces mots se sentit malade et ne put
aller plus loin. - ainsi périt le puissant
qui détruit tout pour satisfaire une envie.

So much for Melancholy and Fatality.

MINUTIÆ, a *love of detail,* can be seen in small regular handwriting, of a rather upright character; the stops, and dots, and dashes, will all be carefully inserted in their proper places. Some people may call this a "finnicking" hand, an economical hand. Probably it is economical, because people who enter in detail are generally careful of the pence. We often find compilers in literature writing this careful hand, and when we do we may depend on the individual to do his work neatly and well. The signs of imagination will be absent, as a rule, but occasionally we find the same writer indulging in less detailed penmanship when writing a private note. His press-hand is decidedly distinct from his private caligraphy. This only shows that his work is carefully done, and that he is plodding along in his compilation, not giving reign to his imagination. The usual signs of carefulness will be found in the case of a lover of detail.

The type of MODESTY is to be found in the sizes of the capital letters relative to the smaller ones. Speaking of individual letters, at the beginning of this work, we referred to this trait. Those who make the capitals about "half as high again" as the smaller letters, we may decide that the writer is of a retiring and modest nature. At the same time the upstrokes of the capital M should be of the same elevation or nearly so. This equality argues an absence of Pride and consequently the presence of Modesty and self-effacement, particularly if the strokes be close together.

MUSICALLY inclined people, and MUSICIANS, show signs of Imagination, Tenderness and Sensitiveness, sometimes Sensuousness. Nor is this unnatural. Music is the language of the soul, and likely to stir the feelings and imagination deeply. We also find originality in musicians, so we may be on the look out for quaintness of capitals, eccentric letters also at times, but generally tenderness and gracefulness are most evident. We can give a few illustrations of different composers.

In composers and actors and actresses we nearly always find a little flourish after the signature. This gives us to understand that the composer or actor has a desire for praise and appreciation which, under the circumstances, is only natural. We have frequently remarked the same trait in literary men who write books and novels, not journalists simply.

Here are the signatures of two musicians, Gretry and Boieldieu. The latter autograph is taken from the last letter ever written by the author of "Dame Blanche," another instance of the failing writing. There is much tenderness in the sloping hand, and still more tenderness in the "tender kisses," which close the letter. There is clearness in the spaced words and lines, imagination in the terminal *e* of *ie*, in the ascending bar of the *t*, and in the capital initial of his name. The flourish is also present—

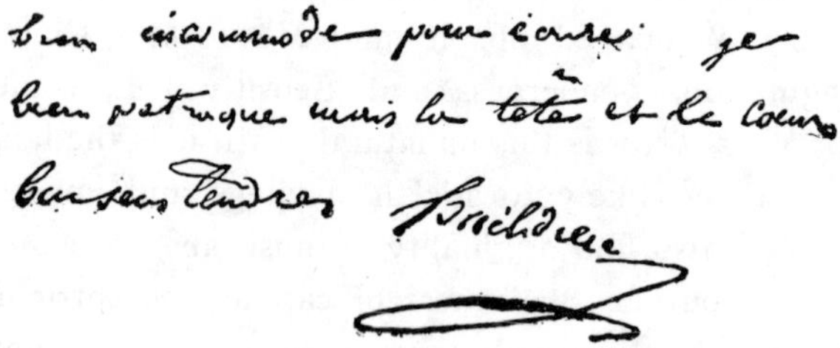

The autograph of Gretry shows will and perseverance. The writing is inclined and the G imaginative.

The autograph of Sir Arthur Sullivan is distinguished for gracefulness, tenderness, and a certain sensuousness, with considerable originality in the A. Here, again, is the flourish. There is much energy in this signature, connected ideas, and taste.

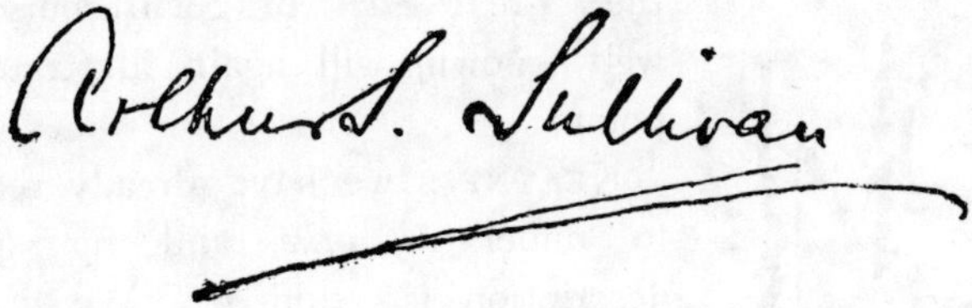

Sir William Sterndale Bennett, which is the next musical

name on our list, is very refined. His writing is said to have a resemblance to Mendelssohn's. There is no flourish, however, but great talent and imagination.

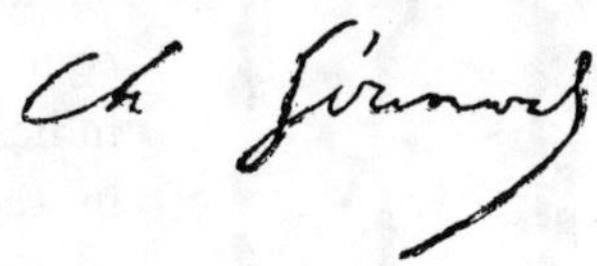

Gonoud's signature is clear and original, with an imaginative tail to a clever *d*.

III.—Of Nobility, Neatness, Obstinacy, and Order.

Nobility of character and a certain grandeur will be found in the large and "magnificent" writing already alluded to. *Noblesse oblige* is a well-known proverb, and frequently we see the nobility—the aristocracy—writing fine bold hands, clear honest rather magnified penmanship, but certainly indicating the noble traits of human nature. There is a simplicity and clearness in this noble writing which is exemplified in the hand of the late General Gordon, in that of the statesman Sir Robert Peel. Lord Palmerston wrote a clear but diplomatic hand, while the signature of

the "great Earl of Shaftesbury," so well known, will again illustrate our points.

NEATNESS we have already referred to under *Minutiæ*, and no special description is required. We can all recognise a neat writing in its careful appearance, its tidiness, and regularity.

Passing on from these obvious characteristics, we come in our alphabetical order to OBSTINACY, which has almost as many degrees as Will (*q.v.*). Of course, the first thing to look for is the indication of Firmness, and the decision in the writing; the crossing of the *t*'s particularly being characteristic, and often a heavy writing, and generally rather upright. Sometimes we find a hopelessly dull determination in writing, iron-like *rigid* lines, but your ordinary obstinancy is shown in the thick bars to the *t*'s, as in the words annexed, which is a thoroughly obstinate type. And see, also, Despotivity, already explained.

The next is an English specimen just as obstinate. Perhaps the hand may have altered since the lady sent me the letter from which the line is taken—

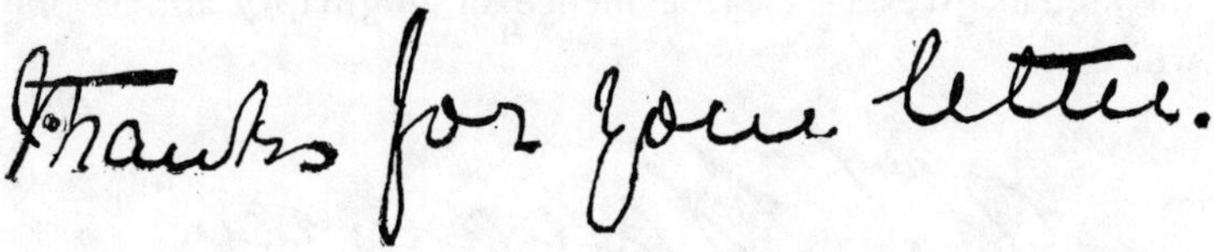

There is also a fine amount of obstinate determination in the signature of Doctor Livingstone. Here we have tremendous power and dogged resolution. Readers who have followed the indications of Graphology will have no difficulty in reading the characteristics of the celebrated traveller—

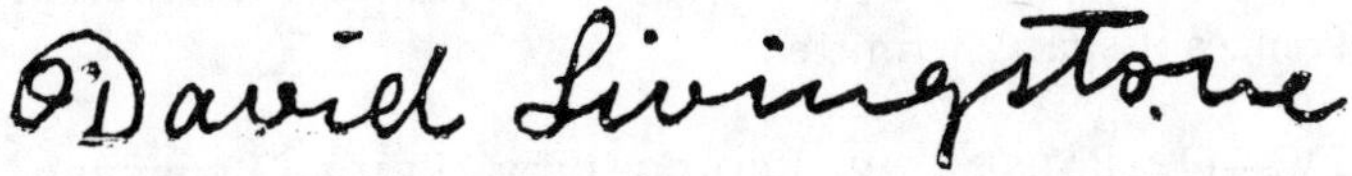

When the *t* is crossed in an upward direction, not in the tenacious manner shown above, we will find the writer is rather irritable in his obstinacy. The bar is more inclined to fly away at times, and intellectual energy may then be predicated. When the cross of the *t* is crushed down on other letters, we find a most dogged obstinacy and autocratic will. (See also under Will, and Perseverance.)

ORDER and ORDERLINESS, like NEATNESS, can be seen at a glance. We have even writing, all the stops rounded nicely, and the *t*'s crossed carefully. We shall find the lines even, the margin well marked, and general signs of care ; no negligence.

ORIGINALITY is another easily detected trait. We find eccentric capitals, a peculiarity of form, and signs of imagination. Very often a queer flourish, or an abnormal terminal letter, will indicate originality. The autograph of General

Cavaignac gives us clear evidence of originality and strong will.

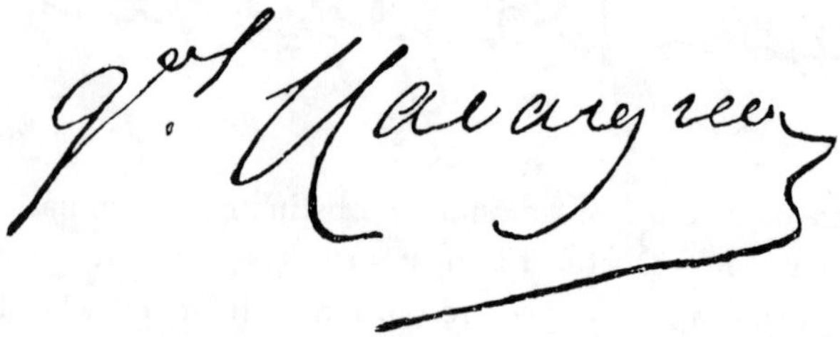

The signatures of Richard Wagner, Emile Zola, Lord Tennyson, Professor Ruskin, and many other celebrities show considerable originality, and it would be easy to multiply instances if space permitted.

IV.—Of Parsimony, Prodigality, Pride, Perseverance, Reserve, Etc.

Parsimony is a vice which may be deemed economy in excess, and we must look for the signs of avarice in our investigations for Parsimony. As when considering the signs of economy and avarice we gave certain specimens of handwriting, it is not necessary to give any more. We know the close-fisted avaricious penurious style which objects to any expenditure of paper and ink beyond that absolutely necessary for the writings. "Close-fisted" has its application to penmanship as well as to the hand itself.

Penetration is a gift which will be found if some care be bestowed on the caligraphy. It is not a virtue worn upon the sleeve. Of course it can easily be detected in the face, but in the writing it is not so easily found, though the united letters and words will put us quickly on the track. The salient type of penetration is *angularity*, not only in the small letters, but in the capitals, in which the *angular* forms take the places of the rounded curves. The separation of letters added to this angularity, will give us great penetration and observation. Something of this may be perceived in the autograph of Professor Huxley, who writes in a rather angular style. When writing of the critical faculty, we also gave some specimens, and penetration will generally be found to accompany the separated style. See the signature of Th. Gautier, page 45 (ante.).

PERSEVERANCE has well been termed "an active Patience." Patience and Perseverance are virtues which we should all like to possess. PATIENCE is calm in its straight lines and general evenness of writing. We can all understand that a calm and patient person will write a hand in which no signs of irritability will be observable. In a persevering handwriting there will be more energy and rather long bars to the *t*'s—a firm and decided caligraphy, withal. There may, in a patient hand, be signs of Imagination, Tenderness, Benevolence, and so on; in fact, the two latter characteristics are generally existent in the patient mind, but we shall not find any tokens of anger or impulsive action, no fly-away bars, and so on. The evidences of will and determination are not too great, but decided; not thick and heavy, but gently firm, and the lines of the writing straight, sometimes of a slightly upward tendency.

PERSEVERANCE, as already remarked, is energetic, more angular, with long decided bars to *t*'s, showing will, and ending often in a thicker line than the bar began with. Some writers say that the cross-bar ends in a decided "hook" or throw-back of the stroke, but this I have not particularly noticed. The *determination* of the long cross-bar, often thicker at the end than at the beginning, is a decided characteristic of Perseverance. The autograph of Marshall Pelissier appended shows this tenacity, energy, and perseverance.

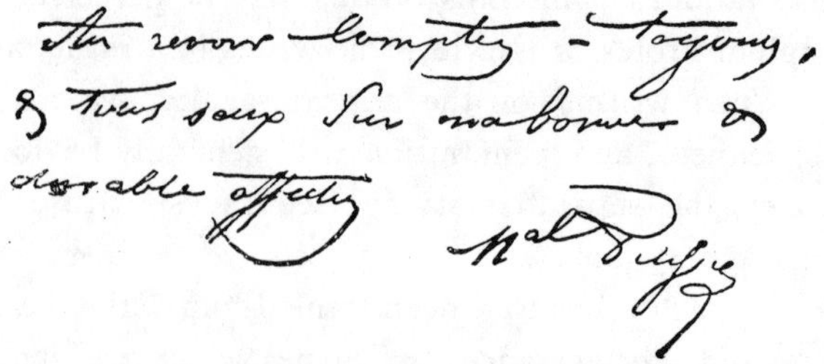

POETIC FEELING is most frequently seen in the clear artistic capitals something like printed letters, and also in the imaginative and lengthy upstrokes and downstrokes of certain letters, *h*'s, *d*'s, *y*'s, *g*'s, etc. There are, of course, poets and poets. Some of a sensuous, some of a more ethereal nature. Some therefore write more heavily than others, thus

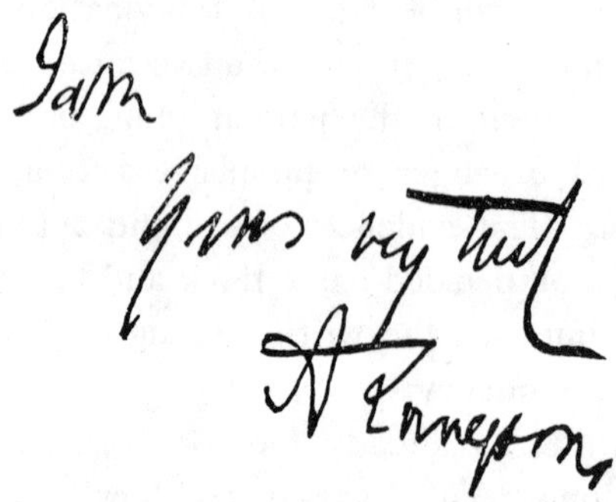

indicating a more voluptuous temperament, and a love of ease in life. Some write tender sloping hands of the sentimental and romantic order—some more upright, indicating a better business habit and a certain care for "No. I" (themselves), with all their poetic feeling and execution. Imaginative capitals are general. Sometimes the writing ascends, here is impulse, and even enthusiasm; if the handwriting fall we may expect a rather melancholy tendency of composition. The sensitive poet will slope his writing—Lamartine wrote thus—

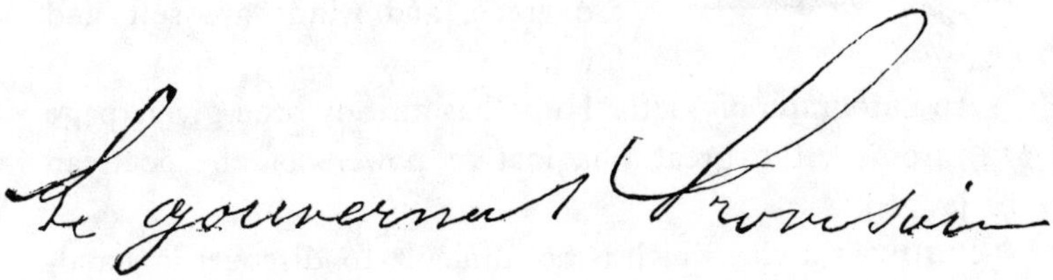

Look at the signature of Oliver W. Holmes. Here is gracefulness, tenderness, and enthusiasm, caution, care, and artistic taste, as well as real poetic feeling.

Longfellow's autograph is decidedly disappointing. It is upright, by no means so tender and sentimental, nor so impulsive as one would expect. There is a want of spontaneity about it, as if it were almost a task to "turn out" poetry, as if his work were a labour—even if a labour of love.

It is imaginative and artistic, careful, clear, but without the tenderness of "Owen Meredith," and of Oliver Wendell Holmes. Those who knew Longfellow intimately, may be able to throw some light on his caligraphy. There is certainly an adaptation to different styles in his writing, as there is in Mr. F. Locker's hand, with a love of physical ease, as if, indeed, it were very pleasant "to lie amid some sylvan scene," when "woods are green, and winds are soft and low!"

Locker's writing

An autograph of Victor Hugo has already been given (page 72), from it the great imaginative powers of the poet can be judged.

PRIDE is a vice which is not difficult to discover in handwriting, but a distinction should be drawn between the arrogant pride, and what is termed "proper pride," which is only self-respect. This latter is observable in nearly all writing; in every gentlemanly or ladylike hand, as a matter of course; and is perceptible in the M's and N's. The first stroke of the letter M, whether it be formed of two or three strokes, will be higher than the succeeding one. This indicates a "proper pride," a self-respect, and perhaps self-esteem!

The haughty domineering pride will be discoverable in the arrogant and pretentious caligraphy, in which large and small letters are, to use an "Irishism," all of the same size, or perhaps it should be said in which the small letters assume almost capital proportions, and the large letters are increased in size. Frequently we shall find in these efforts of penmanship a tendency to selfishness and self-appreciation—egotism, in fact. Then, naturally, a haughty disdain for our fellow-creatures will be assumed, as any one with a very high opinion of himself is apt to despise others. This is the worst kind of pride—a contemptuous and disdainful pride. Very clever people may exhibit this trait equally with the comparatively unintellectual, and the very curling small *d* will betray it.

PRODIGALITY has been touched upon in our remarks concerning extravagance, and the application of the test indicated in a former chapter will suffice for a kindred weakness. A wastefulness or unnecessary expenditure of ink and paper, and a large pretentious style of writing, flowing and extended letters, want of punctuation and orderliness, will give us the required clue. Other indications will appear, of course, and may greatly modify the actual verdict as regards Prodigality, *per se.* For instance:

We may, and frequently do, find care and caution displayed, even a selfish tendency may be shown. If so, we must apply the antidote, and argue out the disposition, whether a prudent expenditure is there—that is, an extravagance which will not "outrun the constable," and a selfish *personal* prodigality, a spending of one's means, chiefly for one's own enjoyment. In the first instance we may decide on Generosity rather than Prodigality, and in the second the inference is obvious—a selfish spendthrift.

In all cases the student must read between the lines of the writing, and weigh the various indications against each other. This you may declare is absurd; but when it is remembered that human nature is made up of contradictions, the necessity for a close analysis will be acknowledged. There are degrees in all attributes, and saving clauses in every disposition. If we are aware of our weakness we can check it. We may have something more to say about contrasts and contradictions by-and-by, if space permit.

QUICKNESS of thought may be referred to Impulse and

Imagination, with the signs of Penetration; there is an energy in the writing and the traces of Versatility (*q.v.*).

QUARRELSOME people write irregular and rather angular hands, with flying up corner to the *t*'s.

REFINEMENT is ascertained in penmanship by the gracefulness of the capital letters, and a delicate clearness and distinctness in the writing. We shall also find the signs of tenderness developed, with a general neatness in the arrangement—no coarseness nor thickness, and not too much imagination. Any one can judge of elegance and grace of penmanship; and in these indications lie the foundation of the refinement we should expect in the writer; the calm neatness is very characteristic.

RESERVE in handwriting is discoverable by the closing of the *o*'s, *a*'s, the lower parts of the *d*'s, etc. No one of a self-contained and "ungushing" disposition ever keeps the loops open. There are degrees in this trait also. We find some *o*'s closed, perhaps some open, some *a*'s unclosed, and so on. This would indicate a chatty pleasant nature, a conversational person, but one who would not wear his or her heart upon the sleeve, nor be really confidential unless sympathy were sought for consolation's sake and for self-gratification; this, in particular, if the writing be rather upright.

CHAPTER V.

On Selfishness and Sensitiveness, Sensuousness, Sensuality, Simplicity, Sincerity, and other Characteristics, Alphabetically Considered.

THE great-god SELF is the leading motive to be considered in this chapter. From the SELFISHNESS, pure and simple, through the various stages of Self-appreciation and Self-devotion, we must pass to other traits. Some have been referred to in preceding pages, but we will treat them all as briefly as possible, consistently with clearness.

"Am I selfish?" is a question which many people have put to the writer of these pages, and which, I daresay, many of my readers have put to themselves. They can find out by a glance at their unstudied writing. Does it stand upright? and do the capitals, such as C, M, N, E, and other letters curve back inwardly? The upright hand is written by people who look after themselves first, who may be affectionate, even capable of strong passion in love, who will show their affection, too, and be very greatly *epris* with the members of the opposite sex who enchain them; but only so long as they are amused and interested. This class of upright writing is generally heavy and sensuous, showing a fondness for mundane amusements. Beware, trust her not, or him not, who displays affection in such a hand. It will not last, it will amuse itself, it has no tenderness, it is hard, and severe ; and crushing when the object no longer pleases.

Again, the writing may show some refinement, with softly-rounded curves, rather heavy strokes, and selfish curves. Here, again, is no true tenderness of soul. There is liking, and, perhaps, friendship in the person's manner, but it will not go far. So long as you are amusing and pleasant, he or she will like or love you, but when you fail to amuse or to contribute to his or her amusement, the individual will cease to care, and Selfishness will seek a new "chum" in the absence of the former. Such people are always ready with excellent reasons—moral reasons, generally—for relinquishing their friend or lover, either it "isn't proper" now, or they have scruples concerning Mrs. Grundy, etc. This is mere hypocrisy and selfishness, because, after a while, you will find them flirting with, or cajoling another victim in the same way Unfortunately, the female sex is the one most liable to these vagaries, though men are by no means free from equally selfish traits.

Even when the writing exhibits tenderness (in the sloping style), and when we find the curves of the capitals already mentioned, and perhaps a compressed, close, hand, selfishness will be present, and the individual will be exigent, and very likely jealous. If the writing be thick, the passion of love will be accentuated, and the jealousy, perhaps, increased. Angular and upright writing and inward curves indicate a cold-hearted selfishness which is akin to cruelty if the will be determined. I am sorry to say I have three specimens of this writing before me now—two from ladies—and though I cannot in fairness produce them, they are very characteristic.

SELF-SUFFICIENCY is exhibited in curling *d*'s, as in the

specimen annexed. This form shows great self-appreciation and self-sufficiency. The accompanying specimens of these flourishing small *d*'s give the exaggerated form of this trait of character. The press-hand of Madame George Sand has a similar distinction. She wrote two

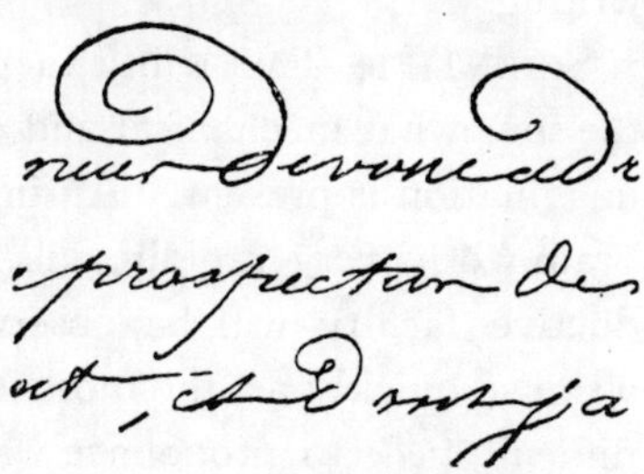

styles, but even her ordinary hand was not free from a certain self-appreciation or vanity. However, it will not suffice to pin our faith absolutely upon the more or less artificial writing of Madame Dudevant, who strove to write a masculine hand, and assumed a masculine character, even

in dress ; but her writing displays a singularity and a species of vanity, nevertheless. The down strokes, like the *d*, betray vanity and self-assurance.

SELF-DEVOTION is an attribute to which we referred when mentioning Loyalty. The ascending writing, with high letters, which show enthusiasm and energy with an absence of any signs of selfishness, give us the signs of devotion. We shall also find tenderness and sympathy developed in the sloping characters.

SELF-CONTAINED people close up the letters, the loops of the *a*'s, the *d*'s, *g*'s, etc. The same signs as in Reserve will be found in this attribute of character, in a close and upright writing.

SCIENTIFIC TASTE in exact sciences may be opined from the somewhat mechanical and orderly writing when not much imagination is present. An imaginative *savant*, a man whose brain works very rapidly, will not write so neatly. The deductive faculty will be observable. The naturalist will not write so quickly as the more abstract scientist. It is a very difficult task to pronounce with certainty upon the absolute *practice* of science, but the taste for investigation may be deduced from the qualities of penetration, observation, and intelligence. There is an exactitude about the writing of a philosopher, even if his caligraphy be not altogether elegant, a rigidity which tells of mathematics.

Renan *Buffon*

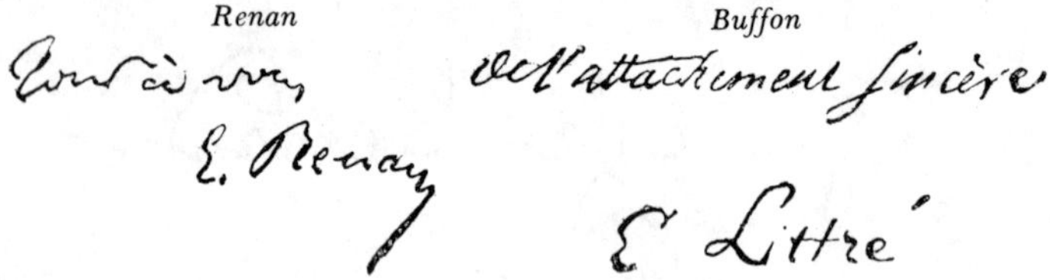

Above are three specimens of *savants'* writing—Renan, Buffon, and Littré—three very celebrated men in their several walks in literature; but mark the difference in the writing: Renan, the Oriental scholar, with his originality, his clearness of mind, his penetration, and *finesse*. There is strong tenacity in the flourish to the name, or rather in the bar which descends from the signature, critical to a degree, and of restless energy. Buffon, the naturalist, is more tender, and still persevering; patient genius, intelligent, neat, and orderly. M. Littré, of the French Institute, of great critical power and much observation, intuitive, careful, prudent, lucid in his ideas. All these men were scientific, but each in a different path; while they had many traits in common, they diverged in character and tastes.

SENSITIVENESS is indicated by the sloping writing of excessive tenderness. Such people are frequently "touchy," and apt to think themselves slighted when there is really no reason for their fears. They think themselves unappreciated, and seek sympathy from their friends, particularly if they are not very strong-willed, and are romantically inclined. The annexed specimen of a lady's displays much sensitiveness and tenderness. There are many kindly qualities in the writing, with considerable energy. The writer is personally unknown to me.

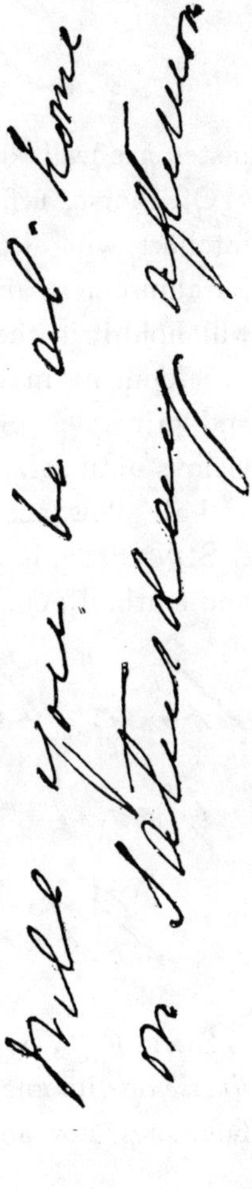

SENSUALITY and SENSUOUSNESS are traits of character which are not both found in the last specimen. There is a great and wide gulf between these characteristics. The former is grossness, the latter a love of beauty in form, and soft ways in life—pleasant, but not gross indulgence. A love of nature, of music, of lawful moderate mundane enjoyment and ease. Most poets and artists display, as well as musicians, the sensuousness of temperament. Witness the writing on page 93, the rounded curve of rather thick down-strokes (Gounod).

SENSUALITY is shown by very heavy writing, the sensual *gourmet*, the lover of good living, will write more uprightly than the man whose affections are dominant. Generally, your sensuous person writes a hand of almost unchanging thickness and strength. Mirabeau wrote such a hand, and his tastes are well known. There is originality in his signature.

Of course, a firm will and other indications of mind and intellect, will alter the ideas of the character ; but the taste for amusement and ease will be existent even if the mind and will hold it in check. The tendency may be present, but its development may be hindered and prevented by resolution and principle. So do not put a person down as sensual or vicious until *every* indication of his writing has been studied, and all allowances made.

SINCERITY, is visible in the following open, honest, clear, and truthful penmanship.

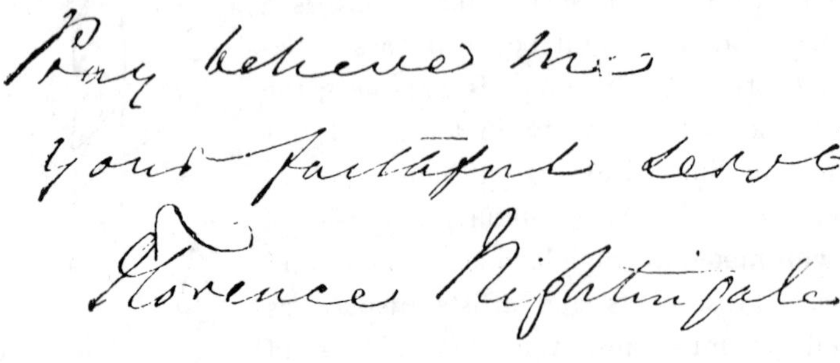

SIMPLICITY is shown in an open clear hand, even, without *finesse* or diplomacy, frank and honest writing. There are no flourishes nor any indication of vulgarity or ostentation.

There is often a boldness in the caligraphy, a sign of bravery, one who has nothing to fear.

SPONTANEITY, quickness of ideas, is found in the imaginative hand, with rather flying crosses to the *t*'s, and movement in the writing, the letters being perhaps of different heights, which presupposes a certain versatility of mind and rapid change of thought. There are, perhaps, also signs of haste and energy.

"Spiritualistic" people write a hand quite opposed to any Sensuality of character—a fine delicate hand.

SUPERIORITY, or the assumption of it, will be seen in the egotistical capitals and somewhat pretentious style of the writing. Pride will be seen, and some disdain.

The indications of STRUGGLE IN LIFE can be seen in the sometimes rising, sometimes falling penmanship. Thus, a person may commence with considerable energy and firmness, and then fall away to rise again, perhaps, in the next line. This indicates the warfare of Will against physical weakness, the struggle to maintain the original force—the willing spirit and the weak flesh. Many readers no doubt have seen such writing. Sometimes it is allied with Despondency and Melancholy, but in all cases within my experience, in which the mounting and subsequent falling character is evident, the struggle between mind and matter is taking place. The mental energy seeks to dominate the physical weakness, either temporary or confirmed.

As explained under MELANCHOLY, the descending writing indicates sadness and chagrin, want of strength to struggle, or want of force of character.

It is unnecessary to give a specimen of such a handwriting, as any one can recognise the symptoms without assistance.

We will give further illustrations in another chapter, only here reminding our readers to balance and weigh the various indications before giving a decided opinion.

Note.—Since writing the foregoing, I have found a specimen which so exactly illustrates the argument, that I annex it.

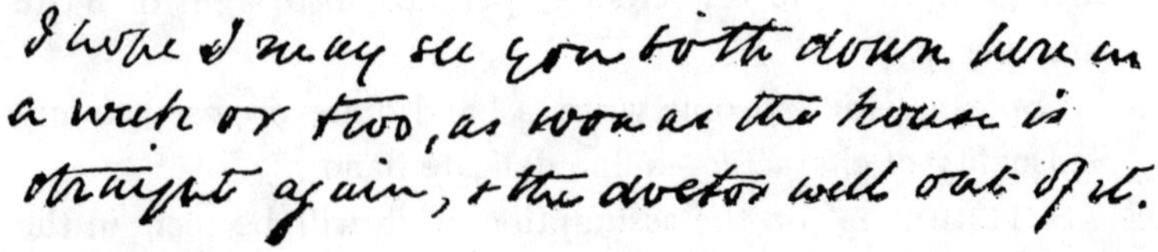
I hope I may see you both down here in a week or two, as soon as the house is straight again, & the doctor well out of it.

This displays the characteristics I have attempted to describe : the struggle, the energy, and the weakness.

CHAPTER VI.

OF TACT, TENDERNESS, TENACITY, TEMPER, AND THRIFT, TRUTHFULNESS, AND ITS OPPOSITES. VANITY, VERSATILITY. WILL, AND WANT OF WILL. WEAKNESS, ETC., ETC.

TACT has much the same appearance as Diplomacy, but is not so greatly accentuated. We have, I daresay, often noticed a rather undulating form of writing, clear enough, but not quite even, not putting a line for two or three letters, but certainly not quite straight. This undulation means Tact. If it be very marked it means Diplomatic reserve, " throwing dust in one's eyes."

Under the heading of *finesse*, in the earlier part of this volume, we have spoken of tact; it is accentuated and developed in its meaning by the will and determination, and a going direct to the object aimed at, without the delicacy of tact. Tact is indicated, then, by straight lines, and rather unequal letters, there is no deceit and dissimulation in the writing, and though some letters may be indistinct there is no intention to deceive.

TEMPER, by which we mean quick temper, is shown in the angular letters and in the hasty flying bars to the *t*'s. We have also signs of Will and Obstinacy, often an ascending and a very firm writing. The "pig-headed" temper, with obstinacy, is shown by the thick crossed *t*'s, and often the return stroke to the cross-bar. (See ANGER.) Good temper is indicated by the evenness of the caligraphy and the gentleness of the writing with considerable self-control—modified will power. We often find energy associated with quick temper and hasty, angular, writing.

TENACITY, like Determination, Firmness, and many such characteristics, is allied with Will, to which we will come in due course. The long stroke to the small *t*, a somewhat thick bar, will give us Tenacity, something after the manner of Perseverance, although more determined, more firm, more angular, indicating greater force if not so much passive endurance. A dogged tenacity.

TENDERNESS has been so frequently mentioned that scarcely any further description is needed. The tender soul is affectionate, sympathetic, and generally sensitive. To find Tenderness we must look for these signs in the sloping writing and kindly curves. The long strokes are indicative of imagination, so in the specimen annexed we find all tender womanly attributes, sensitiveness strongly accentuated, indeed, but kindly sympathy, imagination and generosity.

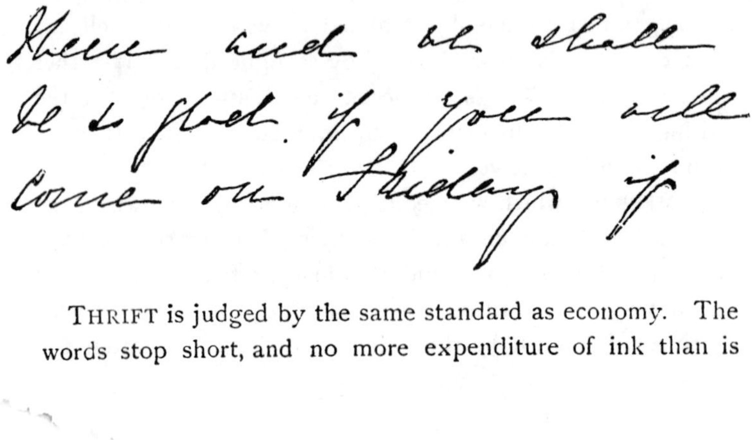

THRIFT is judged by the same standard as economy. The words stop short, and no more expenditure of ink than is necessary is evident. The writing annexed gives us a very good idea of thrift. There is no meanness in it, but decided economy, thrift, carefulness and self-restraint. Sometimes we find the final strokes of letters are angular instead of rounded upwards. This is another indication of thrift—for generosity indulges in rounded ascending finals and curling tails to *g*'s and *y*'s—tails which, instead of turning to the left and then upward, turn to the right upward; not crossing the down stroke, but running to the right of the *y*, and curving gracefully. This writing is decidedly thrifty.

TRUTHFULNESS. We now come to a very important characteristic which will be almost self-evident. Truth has no fear, no wish to conceal anything; and, consequently, the perfectly truthful candid person who is even free from *finesse*, writes a perfectly clear open hand. Compare CANDOUR, in previous portions of the book. The letters are nearly always of the same size, even lines, and frequently the loops of the *a*'s, *g*'s, etc., are open. This is almost gushing Candour, and simple Truthfulness; such a person will tell the whole truth, and if there is little will-power, may make damaging confessions.

Untruthfulness in all its stages may be gauged readily enough after a little practice. Being aware of the signs of Truth, we have only to find them absent, and discover a tendency to Falsehood, Inaccuracy, Exaggeration and Misrepresentation. We all know that people who possess much imagination are never very accurate in their descriptions. They often embellish their narratives, and give a highly-coloured picture, instead of plain facts. In this case we must not look for the sign-type of untruth—we must not expect to find words formed into lines or letters almost purposely hidden, we must look for short spear-like terminations, probably a rather tactical, and certainly an imaginative hand with high and long loops.

The really untruthful person—that is, one who deliberately deceives you, and wishes to swindle you somehow or other, one whom you ought not to trust—is he who writes an indistinct and purposely indistinct hand. He who runs letters into a line with the pen ; who will form four letters in a word with fair distinctness and let the remainder be represented by a wavy stroke. This is untrustworthiness. The ill, or non-formed, letters give us the wish to conceal something, the irregularity of the letters give us *finesse* and diplomacy.

Of course, the straightness of the lines will bear a favourable interpretation if such rigidity and straightness exist. Some people who write kindly, gentle, good hands, display a certain amount of untruthfulness, or *reverse* of the truth, rather. They keep back statements, and gloss over faults from a feeling of good nature, generally ; but these same people would, if questioned seriously, boldly tell the truth. Such people's writing is shortened at the terminals, and a trifle indistinct at the ends of words. (See in THRIFT above.)

Precaution must be taken to distinguish between the truly imaginative writer and the untruthful person. As we have explained, many imaginative authors write very *indistinct* hands, but they do not endeavour to *conceal* their thoughts—all the letters are there, but very quickly formed, not a mere line.

Experience unfortunately leads one to the unpleasant conclusion that comparatively very few, if any, people *always* speak the exact truth. I do not mean that they *intend to deceive*, but they fence with truth, their imagination is aroused, and they will describe an incident with such vivid and imaginary details that you are really deceived. The effect is just the same as if deliberate falsehoods were told. How often do we hear that So and So's remarks must be accepted with the proverbial grain of salt. There is a looseness of statement generally in vogue, misrepresentations are prolific everywhere. Some men—even in high places—distort facts for party purposes: some in private life disguise and represent in a totally different light the circumstances of a case. Whether for tact's sake, for diplomacy's exigencies, for *finesse*, for wish to shield friends, for social purposes, for "business" purposes, for sheer love of misrepresentation, from a wish to hide one's thought, for gain and profit or to cause loss, to excite sympathy, or cause anger, "for fun," and many other reasons, Untruth is almost universal in one form or another, and is found in a very large proportion of the writings of all classes of individuals.

We are now nearing the end of our list of characteristics, and VANITY claims some attention at our hands. This little human weakness is most evident in flourish beneath the signature. A person may have reason for his excellent opinion of himself or herself, and possess some justification of his or her vanity. Queen Elizabeth flourished her signature finely—and no one will deny her vanity; and self-appreciation is also found in the back-curling *d*'s.

The flourish may also indicate great imagination, but in any case it suggests some vanity. The appended autograph of Cervantes, author of "Don Quixote," shows great imagination, but some vanity. There is more "go" in it than in the merely vain flourish. As a rule much flourish may be accepted as an indication of egotism and vulgarity.

There is another kind of flourish which rather argues *impenetrability*, a wish to be secretive. This is when the signature is surrounded by a series of circular sweeps of the pen, as in the case of Flandrin the painter. This is egotism again, and a certain secretiveness, which is, however, accentuated in the next autograph, where the writer is so anxious to be dissimulative as to be also unintelligible to a stranger. The flourish is also close and reserved.

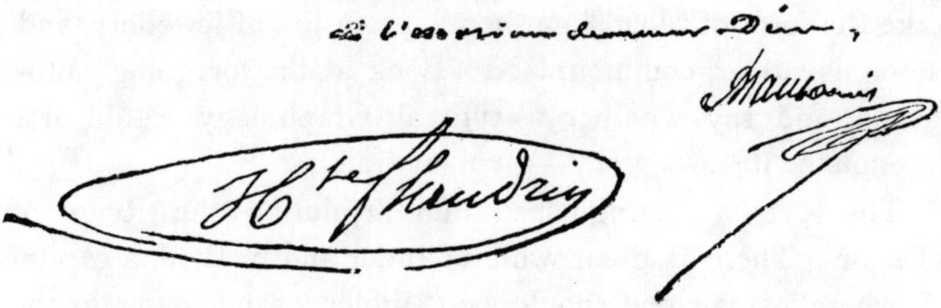

VERSATILITY is accentuated by the different heights and sizes of letters with rounded curves at the ends. There is also some inconsistency in such writing, but we shall find also,

VIVACITY, which is indicated by ascending words, particularly by the quick flying bars to the *t*'s, the open writing, and energetic hasty character of the caligraphy. We can all recognise the vivacious person, and to learn the signs procure the writing of some person who is known by you to be vivacious and versatile. The various indications will then be easily distinguished.

VIOLENCE may be referred to CRUELTY and ANGER.

VULGARITY may be measured by the forms of the capitals, which indicate—if ungraceful—a want of cultivation ; and by the commonplace vulgar flourish, aimless and ostentatious. It is an attempt to be showy, and all such display, whether it

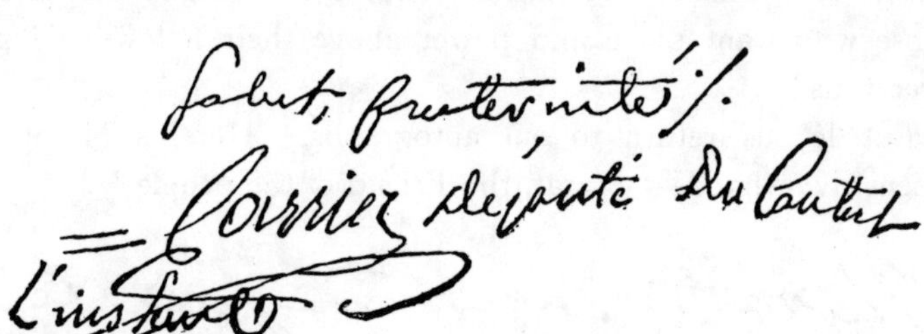

take the form of "loud" garments, profusion of jewellery, and so on, is vulgar, commonplace. Look at the foregoing autograph, and say whether a tyro at Graphology would not pronounce it "swagger"—a vulgar trait.

This person distinguished himself during the Reign of Terror. There is great want of order and method, a capital L where a small one should be. Violence and anger in the angular writing, tenacity and obstinacy and despotism in the strongly barred *t*'s. There are signs of pricks of conscience in the word *fraternité*, in which some letters slope, some are upright. The flourish is meaningless, not imaginative heavy, vulgar, and the back curve of the C is selfish. Students of history may ascertain for themselves whether these indications come near the truth ; but a curious contrast is seen in the writing of Marat, which is gentle and kindly almost, not to say sensitive. This sensitiveness prevented him from witnessing a post-mortem examination, yet his name is the synonym for cruelty! We may refer to this again when treating of Contradictions.

Here are the autographs of these lights of "Liberty, Equality, Fraternity," and the guillotine. What despotism so unreasoning and cruel as the "levelling down" dynasty? Who so intolerant as the advocates of "Liberty and Freedom for all"? Those who shriek loudest for "Equality" are those who want place and power above their fellows. 'Tis ever thus!

But let us return to our autographs. Here is Marat's "sensitive" hand—"Marat, the Friend of the people."

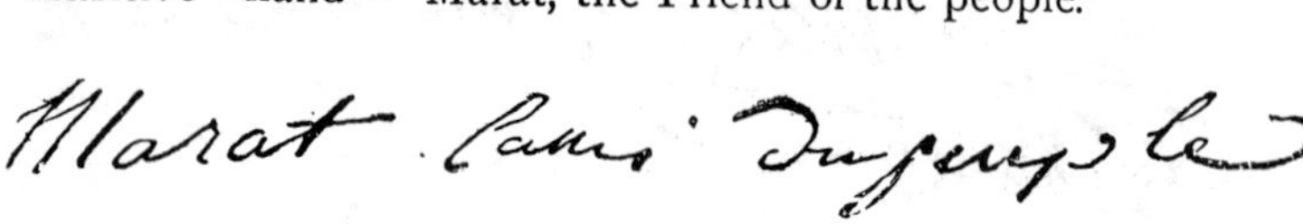

Here are simplicity, force, imagination, talent, a sloping hand, a clear signature. Truly has it been said that an executioner does not change his nature in the exercise of his functions !

We will now pass from these considerations to discuss Will in its various phases.

WILL is perceptible in an almost infinite number of signs and shades, from the strong, cruel, despotic will to the gentle and almost timid protest which gives way at the least opposition. The strength of the cross-bar of the *t*, and the determined bar beneath the signature in writing, is equivalent to the thick topped thumb in Chiromancy. This comparison can easily be sustained, and had we space, we could, and perhaps some day we may, bring forward our reasons and proofs in aid of the argument that certain penmanship is traceable to certain formations of hands ; but at present we cannot enter into this very interesting question. The Will is waiting to be explained, and constrains us to proceed.

We can all judge for ourselves, and from our own writing—in fact, from our own characters—whether or not we are obstinate, despotic, arbitrary, or yielding. There is little need for diagrams here. We have seen under some of the foregoing characteristics, DESPOTISM, DETERMINATION, etc., that the will exists. The general view is of the *t*, but there are many who cannot be suited to a *t* by such a rule, and the many various means of judging must here be considered.

The despot drives his pen with an iron will across the letter, and holds it firmly at the end. There is no flinching from his purpose, the bar is even stronger at the end than at the beginning. Any one who has a collection of autographs of great men who have made a mark in history—even Cromwell, who, though he had no *t* in his name, barred the double *l* strongly—all such men, we repeat, crossed the *t*'s firmly and hard. We have before us an autograph of Prince Bismarck, "the man of blood and iron," as some people call him. His firmness and decision are wonderful in the final *k* of his signature, and in the angularity of it we perceive quick temper, but always force and firmness with, it must be said, a sloping of letters which indicates tenderness beneath his rugged despotism.

But the WILL is accentuated when the *y*'s and *g*'s have no return tails, and end in strong strokes square at the end. These signs are often and nearly always accompanied by a single line beneath the signature, sometimes a very thick line. All these traits exhibit a strong firm despotic will which is still further increased by the cross-bar of the *t*, if it be drawn low on the letters as is sometimes seen. Such a writing gives a most "pig-headed" resolution and inflexible will, such as M. Jules Verne's hero, Keraban, is represented as possessing. These indications, again, are confirmed or lessened by the general character of the writing. For symptoms of Anger we must refer to the previous pages, but when the writing is more rounded than angular and firm, we may modify our decision and expect a very obstinate somewhat weak intelligence. An unimaginative writing will confirm this case in which the *t*'s are *shortly* but *strongly* barred—a very short cross indeed. I have before me such a writing, but it would not be courteous to reproduce it.

When the *t*'s are crossed high, with flying strokes, we have energy and irritability of temper. Sometimes the bars are fined away to a point. Here is yielding after awhile. Sometimes the bar has quite a return stroke—a kind of hook—

and long withal. Here we have perseverance, always supposing the bar be firm.

A thin stroke and no cross at all on the *t* indicates absence of will-power, but we must consider the other letters and the signature, as already remarked, to be perfectly certain as to the entire absence of Will. When the will is well developed, and the writing upright, or selfish, the deduction is not very happy. There is then a coldness of heart which is unpleasant to meet with, and such people will have things arranged with a view to their own convenience rather with reference to other people—unless a stronger will be present, and then the air will get thick for awhile.

These are the most general traits of Will and its phases, and the deduction is easy. A reference to the other characteristics will soon confirm or modify our first impressions.

WEAKNESS, bodily weakness, is shown in the descending character of the writing, either throughout the letter or occasionally. Another sign is a kind of carelessness and want of force in detail when there is abundant evidence of Energy in the writing; but the former may be relied on. More generally, in the energetic hand, the struggle is manifest; some words will be straight, others sloping, and then we shall find that the latter part of the letter is not nearly so well written as the commencement. There is a tendency to slur the words, and this must not be accepted (always) as a sign of untrustworthiness, or deceit. The firmer and truer writing must be compared with the "gladiolated," or amputated forms.

WORRY will also write a despondent and rather irritable hand, sometimes the traces of despondency are very apparent, but a great deal will depend upon the will-power of the individual. Of course, a strong-willed person will endeavour to triumph over his difficulties, and then the signs of worry will be almost obliterated, but here and there we shall find the traces of trouble and anxiety, uncertain letters, and by a deductive judgment arrive at a pretty correct conclusion.

We have now come to the end of our list of characteristics, unless we please to include ZEAL, a trait which is rather allied to enthusiasm and devotion, which we referred to under the head of Loyalty, a pleasing attribute. Whether Zeal is very desirable or not is a matter of taste; Talleyrand thought not. It appeared to him to argue a want of caution, a "gushing," tendency, which is certainly to be deprecated in business and particularly in diplomacy. We cannot find caution allied with zeal, that is a fact. So with this truth, a Graphological as well as an official truth, we will close this chapter.

CHAPTER VII.

Of Contrasts, and some Generalities.

IN preceding chapters we have endeavoured, and we trust with some success, to explain the numerous traits and characteristics of average human nature as indicated by handwriting. But in every hand we must be prepared to find contradictions, opposing tendencies, which may to the learner of Graphology appear unsurmountable difficulties. Concerning these, and a few other points, we shall have something to say here, in conclusion.

Let me give an instance. I, myself, only two days ago was requested as a "great favour"—it is always put in this way—to delineate the character of a lady from her writing; and complied with the (inconvenient) request. It was a curious contradiction. It was artistic in taste, generous in disposition but selfish! Truthful, tender, and affectionate in disposition, but changeable. There were decided evidences of a really chatty, almost gushing temperament, and yet a strong appearance of caution, and of a capability of "taking care of No. 1," as the phrase is, which seemed at first sight incompatible with such frankness and apparent openness of mind.

The fact is—I have the written testimony to the accuracy of the deduction I made—that the lady has a business side as well as a social side. I have no idea who she is, but I fancy she has some literary work, for she has strong literary tendencies, and she may be an art-critic, or writer on decorative art, or such like. At any rate her hand is contradictory, and the only way to arrive at a fair conclusion is to weigh the contrasts and the opposing tendencies which would in the present case indicate a pleasant generous friend, but a decidedly excellent "woman of business," who would hold her own with any friend in *business*, even though subsequently she in friendship made up any difference in a most liberal way.

So we find generosity with a display of caution—as in the case under consideration—caution tempers the tendency to extravagance, and it does not degenerate. Economy may be allied with signs of carelessness, but the medium is found, and prudence or thrift is the outcome of the character.

Sometimes one trait almost dominates the other. Affection may be well developed, and selfishness also. Now, how can we decide on this contradiction. Here we have a decidedly sensuous hand, in which the tendency to love is plain, and yet it shows signs of selfishness and will-power; what should we say of this person? The student of Graphology will be very cautious, and beware of him, or her, who writes such a hand.

He, or she, will be very pleasant, and even affectionate, as long as it suits! If you see no *tenderness*, do not pin your faith to it. The nature is hard, passionate, changeable.

If you perceive tenderness and stinginess in a hand, you need not fear to marry the writer, if a woman. She will be economical and affectionate in her marital relations. This tenderness is the leading characteristic of female hands, and is also very frequently apparent in masculine writing; but at times we meet with the hard-hearted, cold-hearted, and yet passionate, woman who is of all women most to be dreaded, who will sacrifice you to her own pleasure, and cast you aside when done with. She has her prototype in the cruel sensualist of the opposite sex.

There is one essential point in this study—viz., the writing submitted must be perfectly natural. The writer must have no idea when he pens the letter that it will be sent in for examination. We shall then attain an approximate notion of the true characteristics of the writer This is important.

Another contradiction which has come under our notice within a few years is this—Prodigality *and* Stinginess! There is a writing as contradictory as possibly can be, and it was at first rather puzzling. A man—it was a man's writing—who possessed evident tastes for enjoyment of mundane pleasures, with a tendency to extravagance and display, and yet one who was decidedly egotistic and stingy! Here was my friend's difficulty. The writing was submitted to me privately.

"How can you tell me such a character as this? It is a perfect contradiction," said the friend.

"Do you know the individual?" I asked.

"Perfectly well! Have known him for years. What do you make of him?"

"He is rather selfish, fond of pleasure, and good dinners."

"Granted; but how about the contradiction?"

"He is generous to *himself;* he will spend money on his *own enjoyment,* or on those who minister to his pleasures; but he will not give money away. He makes a display of it occasionally. Nevertheless, he has some excellent qualities."

"For instance?" asked my friend.

"He is truthful, clever, possesses excellent judgment, has very clear ideas when he chooses to devote his mind to business. Is amusing, chatty. His faults I have told you: he is a rather *stingy prodigal*, as the Frenchman said, but a good host when he does entertain"

"Well, you're about right," said my sceptical friend, with a half-sigh. "It's rather odd, too. *I wrote that myself.* You've hit me hard, but you're confoundedly near the truth."

This incident actually occurred in a club-room. The conversation being repeated from memory only. The incident is true in all essential points. I confess I was startled, but the individual did not deny the accusations. He was truthful and frank.

Occasionally we find contradictory signs in single letters, but we may take it as the general rule that the more clear and more graceful the writing, the better is the individual, taken altogether, as a whole. Therefore, the more distinctly formed the letters, the greater is the cultivation and intelligence *vis-à-vis* with society and general politeness, and such social gifts.

Of course there are numerous cases in which intelligence of the highest order exists in bearish individuals whose minds, but not their manners, are cultivated. There is the old courtesy wanting in these ungraceful writers, and your well-formed, graceful, firm, perhaps rather sloping handwriting, not too thick, not very thin, will indicate the polite and deferential nature the squire of dames, perhaps, but at any rate a pleasing and refined nature, a nature that will cultivate itself in time, even if it never "sets the temse[1] on fire" by much friction and sifting of brains.

The vulgar mind will display a great deal of flourish. The simple signature is the more gentlemanly. A firm straight

[1] Hand-sieves in former use. Hence the proverb of setting the 'Thames on fire."

bar beneath merely accentuates the Will-power. A little curved flourish shows the love of appreciation inherent in the writer. He or she likes praise when praise is due, and recognition by friends, or others, of efforts, artistic or literary, even a little judiciously administered flattery will please, but any *excess*, any loud praise in the person's hearing, would perhaps be deprecated ; with such a flourish the love of admiration is evident. Authors, actors, actresses, and painters, chiefly display this tendency, harmless enough, but evident in the majority of cases which have come under our notice.

Flourishes need not be further discussed. There are the stops to be considered, and they bear some signification. Heavy stops, like heavy writing, indicate a certain voluptuousness of temperament—perhaps even cruelty if allied with violent bars and heavy writing of irritable tendency. Many stops denote a suspicious character ; you will find such an individual filling up the spaces at the end of his written lines with dashes instead of stops : this may also indicate vivacity and imagination if not long dashes, only elongated stops. Caution, method, and suspicion, are all indicated by stops after initials and signatures.

Precision and attention to detail are evidenced in the care with which *i's* are dotted, *t's* crossed, and stops inserted. The absence of all such signs, of course, point to a rather careless, disorderly, person.

These apparently unimportant details have all a bearing upon the verdict which has to be pronounced upon a handwriting, and no one who desires to become a real Graphologist will omit the practice of studying stops as well as the initial letters, the finals, and the sizes of individual characters in the midst of words.

In our introduction we made some remarks concerning the hands of various writers, and the criticism which has been passed by certain people on Graphology. Many people think it perfectly impossible to delineate character from writing; others are simply incredulous, and *decline* to believe. To such people the following pages, as an Appendix, are addressed, and they may there find the reasons they refuse to recognise. These statements have already seen the light in the pages of a magazine; not very lately, but they serve to bear out our study of Graphology, and will assist the reader. They were originally penned as a reply to an article in another magazine the Editor of which did not "see his way" to insert the reply to the original article. It would be useful if it were permissible to print both articles, but as the points in question are indicated in the reply, the original statements scarcely require to be quoted *in extenso.*

We have now come to the end of our tether. The Grammar of Graphology is written. So far as its application is concerned, there is no difficulty. Any one may very quickly learn the way, but only practice will give the necessary facility. Intuitive perception, as well as the faculty of logical deduction is necessary to enable the student to succeed. Hundreds are surprised to see their friends' characteristics jotted down so plainly, and they will often deny the deductions made, because they do not thoroughly know their friends, or are too loyal to confess the faults they recognise.

Nevertheless, the truth is great and will prevail. The facts are indisputable. We have laid them down, and any one who takes the trouble may easily verify the statements. There is no mystery, no charlatanism. Any reader can test the matter for himself, and we will then be satisfied.

APPENDIX.

The Study of Handwriting.

A CRITIC in a late number of a popular magazine in an article on Handwriting and character, says, "Handwriting lets out secrets . . . but how are we to judge?" The following pages will, we think, indicate the method, and dispose of many of the critic's objections. This essay is from the Graphologist's point of view—not to contradict but to amend the statements of the critic in "Murray."

In the first place, it should be borne in mind that the actual style of writing—I mean writing that is usually termed a "good" (that is, a clear) hand—has comparatively little bearing on character. A man may be as honest as the day and write a "bad" hand, another may be deceitful and diplomatic, and yet write boldly, frankly; and we say what a good hand So-and-So writes. All the Graphologist has to do is to study the form of the letters, the upward, the even, or the downward direction of the lines, the firmness of the crossings of the *t*'s, and he will tell you whether the writer is really frank or not, or whether his bad writing is the result of bodily infirmity, age, or the naturally rapid often almost unintelligible scrawl, of imaginative genius, the result of the brain hurrying off at score, and the tired hand's endeavours to keep pace with it.

Again: the Graphologist can only undertake to deduct true character from the *natural* unaffected writing of the subject; and it is a curious trait in most characters that the signature is almost invariably natural, although the writer may have endeavoured, in some measure, to disguise his "fist." But any one may disguise his handwriting; indeed, Lord Chesterfield declared that "any man who has the use of his eyes and his right arm can write any hand he pleases." Is it not a pity some do not please to write more intelligibly! Still such handwriting is not true; but the character of the writer would be discovered after minute investigation; unless he was a practised dissimulator his letters would betray him in a short time.

As regards the change in handwriting in age, or when weakness of constitution, even temporarily, sets in, we have also something to say. The change which often comes with age is due to change of character in the individual, or to cases in which use is second nature; and, therefore the writing is natural outcome of character and disposition. Failing eyesight will often change a hand, as a whole, but the forms of the letters will tell us whether the disposition is altered; or, very possibly, the consciousness of his bodily infirmity will make a man more careful and prudent in his general work and conversation. He may be unconscious of the change in him while he is writing, but circumspection and the necessity for carefulness are impressed upon his hitherto off-hand and impulsive brain. His hand alters, not because his eyesight fails (for he can, and does, wear glasses), but because his *mind* is impaired by his weakness, and his nerves are answering to the brain!

Once more as regards clerks. Mr. Spooner, whom I have

already quoted, says, "We know how meaningless individual clerks' hands tend to become." The writing of some "has become by constant use an almost purely mechanical process."[1] These statements are capable of emendation. Let me, in the first place, state my belief that clerks' hands are not by any means "meaningless," that is, *characterless*, which is Mr. Spooner's contention. The average clerk writes a clear open hand, neat and orderly in appearance. Why? Because he is not greatly imaginative. He is doing routine work for which nature has moulded him, and because his character is plodding, steady, honest, and not imaginative, his writing is steady, clear; well-formed letters, lines straight, all typical traits of a reliable clerk. He is a clerk because he has these characteristics, he has not these characteristics of writing *because he is a clerk!* Precision and neatness are his natural attributes; his writing shows him to be trustworthy, open, candid, honest, painstaking, neat, and tidy. He is all these, and more, or he would not have been retained in his position. How can such handwriting be characterized as "meaningless?"

Besides, all clerks do not write such careful hands, such "copperplate." Take a youthful energetic correspondent, or a stockbroker's quick, clever, smart clerk, a man of ideas and intuition. Will he write a plodding hand? Certainly not. His writing will be flowing, with high-barred *t*'s, and the letters will be uneven in height, showing tact and a flowing imagination, a quick brain! Compare the man who runs in a groove and the man who uses his brain little outside his groove. They are both clerks, but they indicate their tendencies clearly in their writing. There are, no doubt, exceptions

[1] Mark "mechanical;" no spontaneity in it, no will, no brain?

in which men have been obliged to do duties distasteful, and by will and application have conquered their dislike to plodding; but their writing will break out when they are not in the office, and not writing by "rule and line." Even in the ledger you will see the tendency to hurry on.

Therefore, I maintain that hands are not "meaningless." They all have a meaning and character in them, and characteristics suited to the owners. The business hand may not display any marked eccentricity or any great talent for painting or other form of art, but it will indicate punctuality, order, *finesse*, firmness, some selfishness, most likely, with economy. I have such a handwriting by me now as I write, and though the individual is not a regular business man in trade, he is an excellent man of business if report be true. I have had no means of judging of him in such a capacity save from his handwriting.

As regards the handwriting of boys at school, we read, "In no particular is man more imitative than in this matter of handwriting. A vast majority of people in 'forming' their hand, more or less deliberately copy the writing of someone else, parent or teacher, friend or acquaintance." Then the critic says that a certain type of writing "has run over a considerable number of years through the great proportion of the upper boys in one of our public schools, a stamp of handwriting clearly due to the influence of one particular master."

Now, here, to my mind, Mr. Spooner is arguing against himself. He does not say that *all* the boys write alike, only a certain proportion of them, and the writing is due to the *influence of the master*. Precisely; the master's brain has overpowered the youthful brains of his pupils: his ideas are their ideas for the time being, and as he exerts his "influence," he causes them to imitate him. All, save some independent and original *senior brains*, do as his stronger brain bids them. They write as he does, *at school*, but after? When released from his influence, and when they have become lawyers, doctors, soldiers, or sailors, do they write his hand? No, *certainly not*, unless their tastes are still in harmony with his in after life. Do two people *ever* write exactly alike? No, the schoolboys *may* write *like* their master, because they have little will beyond him, and he has formed their characters for the time; but give them another master, and try! Even on the face of the statement some boys write differently; the master has not the same influence with them; they have more "character" than the others.

Thus, I think the argument as to "meaningless" and characterless writing falls to the ground. The cases adduced by Mr. Spooner will not stand the test from the Graphologist's point of view. By "accident," or by continual associations, people may write alike, but the accident is the accident of similarity of disposition and character, and association will mould one disposition to another. If girls write like their mothers, it is not because they "copy" their mothers' writing, it is because their mothers' characteristics are reproduced in them.

There is a considerable approximation, as Mr. Spooner says, to the man's handwriting, by women of the present day, and he goes on to say that women have "copied" the handwriting of the men. In most cases—save when a lady may be writing business circulars, and adopts, temporarily, a more manly hand—I venture to say that this change is in the *occupations* of women; the change in their lives, thoughts, and is the outcome of higher education, greater cultivation, and in the fact of the women treading on men's heels in every path of life, even outstepping them in many ways! Graphologists maintain that it is much less "external influence" than internal (brain) influence that alters the writing. An artistic, somewhat sensuous, determined, woman will give us rounded graceful capital letters, and thick writing; sometimes eccentric forms of letters, which denote originality of mind, thickly crossed *t*'s, which denote will, obstinacy, and so on. This is the very last woman likely to "copy" anything! Her masculine, original, hand gives us an independent and determined character, which makes her write as she does! The critic hits the right note when he says that "the untidy writing of mathematicians arises from their thought so constantly outstepping their power of expression in words." But if so, surely the copying or "imitative" argument is cancelled! If the brain be admitted to have play in a man, why not in a woman and a schoolboy? Is not this admission inconsistent with previous criticism of the contributor aforementioned.

Literary men, too, of impulsive imagination, and of much energy, often write most indifferent hands: illegible, I mean. Take the late Walter Thornbury, the "Ettrick Shepherd," Macaulay, Byron, Fenimore Cooper, and the living (and long may he live) James Payn. Those men are types of most imaginative and *rapid* writing. Some persons will doubtless cite "George Eliot" as an instance to the upsetting of my argument, but I *fancy*, for I do not *know*, that "George Eliot" did not write in a hurry. She had a splendid imagination, but she (I should judge) did not "dash off" her MS. Her clear writing is expressive of intellect and a carefully produced narrative, not a story thrown off from the quick working restless brain of a sensitive, energetic, perhaps irritable writer.

If any one can compare the handwritings of illustrious personages, he or she will at once perceive how the characteristics of the individual are reproduced. Look at Mr. Gladstone's firm, tenacious, "tactful," rather sensuous, but energetic, quick-tempered writing. His obstinate bars to the *t*'s show despotism; the angularity of the letters quick temper; the undulating writing *finesse;* the thickness of it, firmness, obstinacy, love of enjoyment of a more or less physical character, and so on. Oliver Cromwell wrote a bold, steady, hand; so did the Eighth Harry; and Charles the First a fine open, candid, *weak* hand, irresolute to a degree, while his son Charles wrote a very "dissimulating" hand.

Lord Tennyson, again, is clear and classic. Washington with a manly hand, Moore the poet an easy-going careless running hand, as of a man easily influenced by his surroundings. Wendell Holmes a graceful, finished hand. Mary Queen of Scots an elegant, sensuous hand, gentle, and yet with traces of firmness, though simple. Elizabeth's hand is severe and bold. So instances might be adduced almost *ad infinitum* to prove that the writing is due to the brain, and not to "external" influences, as has been said.

I cannot say that I agree in the dictum that a man's signature is the most conscious, and the "less spontaneous" part of his writing; on the contrary, I fancy it will be found that a man seldom writes his signature exactly the same six times running. Ask any bank cashier, and he will tell you his experience. I believe the signature is the true expression in ninety-nine cases out of a hundred, and for this reason: A man may take great pains to conceal his thoughts in a letter, but having finished and read it, being satisfied, he would not wish to dissemble his signature, and it would be with a natural feeling of relief that he would sign his name—for why dissemble it? His name, written by himself, is always valid; he has no need to alter it, save for bodily infirmity, or for some reason which will not bear investigation, a very unlikely case. It is conceivable that a man may alter his writing as a whole, but why alter his signature only? My own impression is that a person's signature is usually spontaneous, and an excellent index to his character. It varies often in details, a fact which tends to prove its spontaneity. It responds to the change of feelings.

Graphologists do not claim to tell a person's history from their Handwriting So far as I am aware the mental and bodily characteristics are indicated, and then a critic will evolve a very excellent delineation of character from the writing. Of course, practice is required. Whist and billiards require practice. Chemistry and other sciences also. So with Palmistry and Graphology. When one understands the basis of these sciences, the details are only a question of application. Mr. Spooner remarks, "there are people to be found who believe in Palmistry!" If he would study Palmistry he would believe in it too. It is merely because people confuse "Chiromancy" with Gipsy fortune-telling, that they "pooh-pooh" Palmistry and kindred sciences. Those who do not understand are always the most contemptuous critics. But to be a true critic one ought to understand the thing criticised.

I could give instances in which I have told character by

handwriting with correctness, which appeared astonishing to any one who had not studied the principles. And in nations as in individuals. There is a grace in the Italian, and sentimentality; a pride in the Spanish types, an argumentative and self-contained look about German caligraphy, with all its long letters of music and imagination. The vivacity of the Frenchman, and the sturdiness of the average Briton are also observable when the writings are compared.

There is no sex in writing, as we have seen. Sir Arthur Helps said that Prime Ministers have generally been good writers; and surely if haste and business influenced us more than brain, these gentlemen would have been excused if they had written badly. But they wrote well! The Iron Duke, Lords John Russell and Palmerston, Sir R. Peel, and others, wrote well. Surely brain and thought had something to do with such clear correspondence, not "outside influence!"

George Sand adopted a manly writing for press purposes, yet her own unstudied writing had something manly in it. We may likewise adopt a handwriting, but I maintain that given a true, natural, specimen of writing, it is perfectly possible to deduce the general character and disposition. And as regards failures and successes which Mr. Spooner compares, what are the failures? Who can tell what his friend is? Was it not Wendell Holmes who said a man had three individualities: The man as known to himself, the man known to his fellow-men, and the man known to his Maker! This is true as anything can be; and so, when you tell Smith that his dearest friend is a liar, selfish, and tyrannical, he denies it, because *he* thinks Jones charming and frank, his very frankness being a cloak for untruth and meanness. The failures are often only failures *d'estime;*

they are true in fact, though the man himself only knows *how* true! People are very often hypocrites, self-deceivers, and think they can remain undetected! Unless they write a feigned or forced hand—an unnatural hand—they will be patent humbugs to the Graphologist.

Was an open "gushing" nature ever known to close the loops of *o*'s and *a*'s? Was a self-contained person ever known to keep the loops open? Why do energetic, successful men write with an upward tendency, and the weak, the desponding, and the sickly—those who have the germs even of illness present in them—write a descending hand? Why does the Critic divide his letters, and the man of connected ideas keep them together? Why do the romantic and sentimental write sloping hands, with long tailed and headed letters; and the selfish "dock" their loops and write uprightly?

I could give instances and examples of all these, but have already said enough. Handwriting is an excellent guide to character, if the rules of common sense and observation be regarded. Experience is doubtless necessary as in all else, but when experience is gained it will be seen that there is more in Graphology than most people think, or are willing to admit.

THE END.